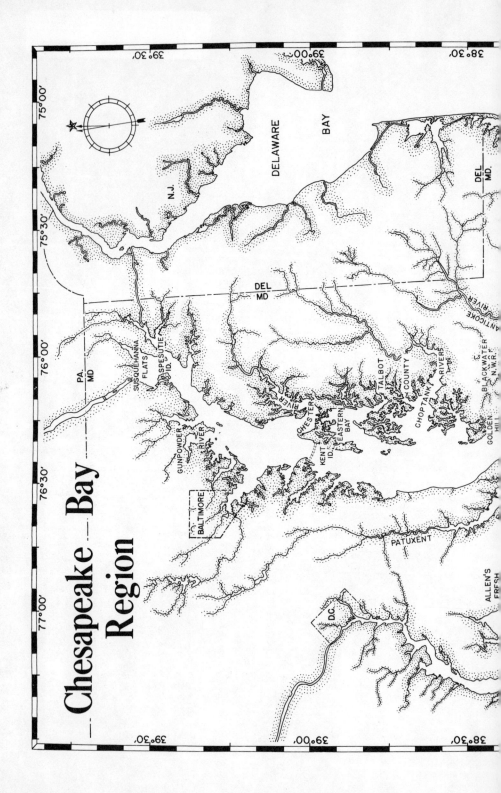

Chesapeake Bay Region

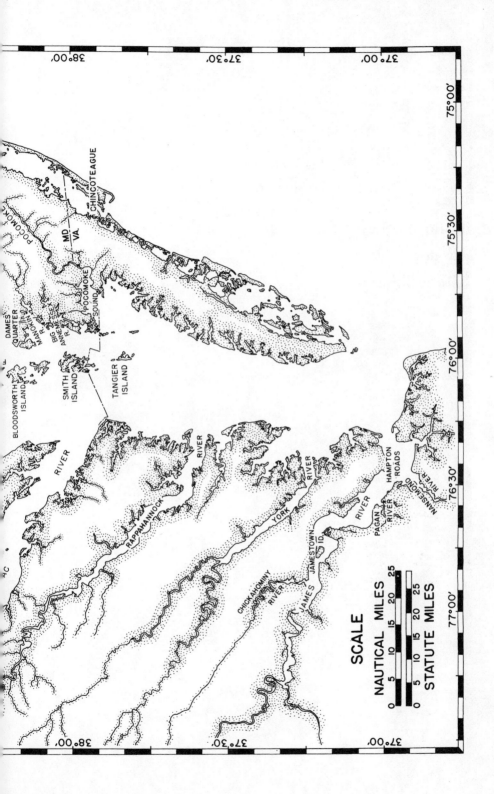

SCALE

NAUTICAL MILES

0   5   10   15   20   25

STATUTE MILES

0   5   10   15   20   25

By Brooke Meanley

Birds and Marshes of the Chesapeake Bay Country
Blackwater
Birdlife at Chincoteague

BIRDS AND MARSHES

OF THE

CHESAPEAKE BAY COUNTRY

Brooke Meanley

Birds and Marshes
of the
Chesapeake Bay
Country

TIDEWATER PUBLISHERS

Centreville, Maryland

Copyright © 1975 by Tidewater Publishers

Library of Congress Cataloging in Publication Data

Meanley, Brooke.

Birds and marshes of the Chesapeake Bay country.

Includes bibliographical references and index.
1. Birds—Chesapeake Bay region. I. Title.
QL683.C48M4   598.2'9755'18   75-17558
ISBN 0-87033-207-4

Manufactured in the United States of America

First edition, 1975; Third printing, 1983

CONTENTS

Appendix

    Common and Scientific Names of:

ACKNOWLEDGMENTS

I am indebted to many of my naturalist friends for permission to use their photographs, for the identification of plants, for technical information, and numerous other favors. I thank them all. Those who have been colleagues of mine in the U.S. Fish and Wildlife Service are Peter J. Van Huizen, Robert E. Stewart, Francis M. Uhler, Neil Hotchkiss, Frederick C. Schmid, Gorman Bond, Matthew C. Perry, John S. Webb, Chandler S. Robbins, Luther Goldman, William H. Julian, Danny Bystrak, Jay Sheppard, James E. Forbes, Morton M. Smith, Don Frankhauser, Rex G. Schmidt, Paul Springer, and Richard S. Posphala.

I wish also to thank John W. (Bud) Taylor for his sketches of a bobolink or reedbird and a swamp sparrow; and bird photographers Sam Grimes, Jack Dermid, Anthony Florio, Hal Wierenga for the use of photographs and Eugene Cronin, Director of Chesapeake Biological Laboratory for the Chesapeake Bay Region map.

My wife, Anna Gilkeson Meanley, often waded through marshes with me, and did much of the editing of the manuscript. I am grateful to her for her assistance.

Photographs are by the author unless otherwise credited.

BROOKE MEANLEY

INTRODUCTION

In the late 1950s, John Webb and I conducted a census of red-winged blackbirds throughout the Chesapeake Bay Country. The census was made during the nesting season and involved tallying territorial males on marshland plots. The plots were selected at random from maps prior to going to the field. By boating up and down most of the rivers and creeks from the head to the mouth of the Bay we learned much about the geography and natural history of Tidewater Maryland and Virginia.

The course of our work led us into waters with such appealing names as the Transquaking, Chicamacomico, Chickahominy, Manokin, and Big Annemessex Rivers; Marshyhope and Chippokes Creeks, and Allen's Fresh; and places with names perhaps less appealing but nonetheless intriguing, like Ape Hole Creek, Marumsco, and Dave's Gut.

Earlier, in the 1930s, I had traveled to some of these same areas with a five-pound camera, wooden tripod, and photographic blind for the purpose of taking pictures of birds. The going was a little tougher in those days. I recall such experiences as taking the Washington, Baltimore and Annapolis train to Annapolis, and at the edge of town hitchhiking a ride in a horse-drawn wagon to Black Walnut Creek to photograph an eagle's nest. On another occasion I stayed awake all night because of the bedbugs in a Kent Narrows boardinghouse. The next day I was to make photographs nearby at a least tern nesting colony where a marina now stands. Many of the photographs and experiences from these and other forays into the Chesapeake Bay Country are presented in this book.

Many birding trips have been made to Chincoteague, and although not a part of Chesapeake Bay proper, it is included as part of the area covered in this manuscript because of its close geographical relationship with the Chesapeake Bay Country. It also seemed appropriate to include brief narratives of the red-cockaded woodpecker, brown-headed nuthatch, and chuck-will's-widow, southern birds near their northern limit that are associated with the maritime loblolly pine forest of the Chesapeake Bay Country.

The following U.S. Fish and Wildlife Service publications have been especially useful in putting together this manuscript: *Waterfowl Populations in the Upper Chesapeake Region*, by R.E. Stewart (1962); *Common Marsh Plants of the United States and Canada*, by Neil Hotchkiss

(1970); *Food of Game Ducks in the United States and Canada,* by A.C. Martin and F.M. Uhler (1961); *Birds of Maryland and the District of Columbia,* by R.E. Stewart and C.S. Robbins (1958); and *Natural History of the King Rail,* by Brooke Meanley (1969).

A book of much historical interest to local ornithologists is *A List of the Birds of Maryland,* by F.C. Kirkwood, published in 1895 by the Maryland Academy of Science. Kirkwood was Maryland's pioneer ornithologist.

BIRDS AND MARSHES

OF THE

CHESAPEAKE BAY COUNTRY

THE PATUXENT RIVER WILDRICE MARSH

The Patuxent River in southern Maryland is a wildrice river. It lies between the Potomac and Chesapeake Bay, and is Maryland's second "oldest" river in terms of settlement by our colonial ancestors. Lord Baltimore's colonists "discovered" Maryland from the north shore of the lower Potomac in 1634.

The Patuxent River marsh has been well known as a sora rail hunting ground of the southern Maryland tobacco aristocracy since colonial times. The river marsh has the richest mixture of aquatic plants of any of the tidal river marshes of the Maryland section of the Chesapeake Bay system.

Fig. 1. Wild rice in bloom. Patuxent River marsh in August. Plants reach height of 8-9 feet in the Chesapeake Bay Country's fresh tidal river marshes.

This variety of aquatics, dominated by wild rice (Fig. 1), is found mainly along the fresh tidal zone of the river, which is about five miles long, and lies between Upper Marlboro and the mouth of Lyon's Creek. The downstream end of the fresh tidal zone is marked by a sharp

Note: Numbers in parenthesis are references to the Bibliography, page 147.

1

transition in the character of the marsh as the water becomes brackish and big cordgrass replaces wild rice.

The wildrice plant of the Patuxent marsh is rather similar to that of the northern Wisconsin and Minnesota lakes where the seed is harvested by Chippewa Indians.

This handsomest of marsh plants reaches an average height of about eight feet in the Patuxent area, but only about five feet in the northern lakes. In the Combahee (pronounced Cumbee) river marsh of the South Carolina Low Country, I measured plants 12 feet in height.

Fig. 2. Francis Uhler, biologist of the U.S. Fish and Wildlife Service, harvesting wild millet in the Patuxent River Valley for use in waterfowl food propagation studies. Photograph by Frederick C. Schmid.

Patuxent wildrice seed is slenderer than that of plants of the northern Wisconsin, Minnesota, and southern Canadian lakes; however, seeds of plants growing along the Cape Fear River near Wilmington, North Carolina, are about the size of the northern variety.

A marsh covered with blooming wild rice is one of the striking sights of the plant world. Along the Patuxent, the golden feathery inflorescence of wildrice plants has developed by early August; and by the first of September the seed is ripe. Seed ripens at about the same time in the northern lakes, but along the Combahee in South Carolina and the Altamaha in coastal Georgia, the seed matures in October.

Wild rice is the dominant plant of the fresh tidal river section of the Patuxent marsh because it occupies broader areas than most of the other aquatics; but, like the other plants, it is found in a particular zone in the marsh.

As reported in *Chesapeake Science* (1), I found such plant zonation particularly distinct in the vicinity of House Creek, one of the tidal guts that winds away from the river up through the marsh. Sedimentation

Fig. 3. Arrowhead is a well-named and common plant of the Patuxent River fresh tidal wildrice marsh.

and washing from tidal action are important factors affecting plant distribution in the marsh. Tidal action deposits sediment along the edge of the creek, resulting in the formation of a low levee usually two or three feet in width. Walter millet (Fig. 2), an important food of rails, teal, and red-winged blackbirds, is the dominant plant in this slightly higher section of the marsh that lies next to the creek. Dotted smart-weed also is found in the levee zone. This is where most of the sora concentrate at high tide, a fact well known to the railbird hunter.

The zone next to the levee strip is lower, and is usually composed of tearthumbs and river bulrush. It is replaced inland by a meadow type with late-seeding rice cutgrass, and in the lowest part of the marsh by nearly pure stands of wild rice. Where washing is not too great, wildrice beds are sometimes found extending up the edge of the creek. Increased sedimentation in a wildrice stand results in displacement by smartweeds.

Plant distribution is also affected where muskrats concentrate their houses, creating "eatouts." Such "eatouts" result in the formation of little ponds in which arrowhead (Fig. 3) and arrow-arum (Fig. 4) are usually the first marsh plants to invade.

Fig. 4. Neil Hotchkiss, Department of Interior biologist and author of several manuals of aquatic plants, stands next to muskrat house made mostly of plants of arrow-arum. Note "eatout" around muskrat house. Patuxent River marsh, Maryland, September 1960.

The luxuriant growth of aquatic plants in the five-mile stretch of the Patuxent fresh tidal river zone reaches the height of seed production between the latter half of August and the first half of September. The seeds of wild rice, smartweeds, and millet are prime foods for the thousands of red-winged blackbirds, bobolinks or reedbirds, rails, and ducks that flock to the area. For most of these birds the Patuxent marsh is a stopover on their southward flight. The peak population of the huge aggregations of birds coincides with the height of seed production.

Local red-winged blackbirds begin moving into the marsh by mid-July, reaching a peak of an estimated 2,000,000 birds by the first week of September. The redwings not only feed in the marsh on the seeds of aquatics, but trade back and forth to the uplands throughout the day where they raid nearby cornfields. At night they roost in the marsh. Unlike the sora rails, bobolinks, and blue-winged teal which begin to show up on the wildrice marsh in August, and which have completed their molt before they arrive on the Patuxent, the redwings, most of which have come from a radius of 50 miles, are just beginning their molt when they reach the marsh.

Fig. 5. Red-winged blackbirds feeding on wild rice. Patuxent River marsh in September. Plants in foreground bordering river are pickerelweed.

Wood ducks, nesting in nearby swamps and bottomland woods, congregate in large numbers on the Patuxent marsh in late summer. The large seeds of arrow-arum are their favorite food, but are repugnant to other waterfowl and marsh birds, probably because they contain calcium oxalate crystals.

Since redwings and bobolinks have more foraging mobility than rails and ducks they have the first chance at the wildrice seed. As soon as the seed reaches the milk stage, redwings and bobolinks begin feeding on it (Fig. 5), and by the time the seeds mature, much of it has been consumed. But some of the seed is scattered to the ground by the wind and activities of feeding blackbirds.

One method used by the redwing to detach seed from the plant is to
fly to the seedhead and while hovering in the air, yank at the seeds.
This tends to pull the plant over, particularly the upper part, so that it
has the shape of an inverted "L." If the plant is bent enough, soras will
jump up and grab any remaining seeds.

The ripened wildrice seed, approximately one inch in length, is long,
slender, cylindrical in shape, and armed with an even longer needlelike
awn, and has a thin hull covered with short, stiff decumbent bristles. A
feeding redwing removes the hull or cover by holding the seed crosswise

Fig. 6. Hunting railbirds on the Patuxent River wildrice marsh, September 1958.

and revolving it in its bill. Redwings feeding on wildrice seed that has
not fully matured acquire a greenish stain on the sides of their bills near
the base.

By mid-September, when the supply of wildrice seed becomes scarce,
redwings and soras feed mostly on the seeds of dotted smartweed,
halberdleaf tearthumb, arrowleaf tearthumb, and Walter millet. The
redwings also are still making forays to nearby cornfields. It was interesting to note that the female redwing, which is smaller than the male,
generally consumed smaller seeds like the millet; while the male fed
more on the larger seeds of the halberdleaf tearthumb. In examining the
stomachs of several male redwings collected in early August, I found
that they had been feeding on the staminate flowers of wild rice.

September on the Patuxent marsh marks the opening of the railbird hunting season (Fig. 6); and the Patuxent wildrice marsh is one of the best known sora rail shooting areas in the country. In the old days the sora was known by the rail boat pusher as ortolan; and the bobolink, then a gamebird, as the reedy or reedbird.

My friend, Percy Blogg, well-known Maryland sportsman of the "good old days," presents an interesting account of the hunting of soras and king rails on the Patuxent in his delightful little book, *There Are No Dull Dark Days* (2). He begins his essay with a poem about the marsh hen or king rail:

"Give me a gun and some old Marsh
Where the pusher's voice calls mark right!
As the king rail springs from the ditch beyond
Then as suddenly drops out of sight.

"Dah he! Mark left! What a thrill as the excited 'pusher' calls the first bird on a beautiful September morn. This is the moment for which the gunnerman has waited many a month. We are on the Patuxent. Everything has clicked: the wind is southeast and gentle, the day warm but not hot. . . . high tide at 7:30 a.m. As far as the eye can see on both sides of the river, artistic stalks of wild 'oats' [wildrice] stand. Over on the higher marshes, a solid mass of brilliant yellow blossoms, called butterweed by the natives, greets the eye.

"Rails, being in good requisition for the table, have been extensively hunted, particularly on the Marshes of the Delaware and Chesapeake bays. Most sought after of the rails is the little sora or Carolina rail. The Virginia and king rail often add variety to the bag, however.

"It is next to impossible to make these birds take wing when they are able to run. Because of this, rail are hunted only when the tide is so high that the flooded marshes afford no shelter and make it impossible for them to run. While the pusher poles a small skiff over the flooded marsh, the hunter stands in the bow, gun in hand. Every now and then a bird will jump, sometimes almost from under the boat, flying away with apparent feebleness, just over the tops of the foliage. As it flies, its legs dangle awkwardly. This ruse, however, is merely to prepare it for the sudden drop which often leaves the surprised hunter drawing a bead on empty space. Ofttimes the gunner does not even see the rail announced by Mark right, Mark left, or simply 'Dah he goes.' "

Another method of hunting rails on the Patuxent marsh when some of us were younger was to walk abreast through the marsh, flushing birds ahead of us. This is tough going because the weather is still hot when the season opens on September 1, and early September is when most of the rails are in. Along with the heat is the muck that one has to plow through, and the jungle of low-lying smartweed with its serrated stems which present the same condition as walking through a brier patch. When we wished to cross a gut or creek at high tide we simply waded in, often up to our shoulders, holding the guns overhead. To make the going a little easier, we discarded boots in favor of tennis shoes.

Fig. 7. Robert E. Stewart, Biologist with the U.S. Fish and Wildlife Service, and sora that he caught by hand while on railbird hunting trip to the Patuxent River wildrice marsh, September 1942.

Walking birds up is an economical approach to railbird shooting, as hiring a pusher costs $15.—$25. a tide. Good high tide shooting lasts about one hour.

On a September morning in 1942, when Bob Stewart and I were walking through the smartweed about a hundred feet apart, I flushed a sora that flew right toward Bob. Bob dropped his gun, reached up and caught the bird (Fig. 7). Soras are slow fliers, but as Percy Blogg says, when they take off, they often drop back down into the marsh before the gunner anticipates that they will.

Fig. 8. Red-winged blackbird banding trap in Patuxent River fresh tidal marsh, near Lyon's Creek, Anne Arundel County.

On the Patuxent marshes in the 1940s, I would flush about two Virginia rails and one king rail to every 100 soras.

As a part of a study of the life history of the king rail, I examined a small series of six stomachs taken by hunters on the Patuxent River marsh in early fall. An interesting assortment of materials was found in this series, including killifish, crayfish, dragonfly nymphs, snails, grass-hoppers, and crickets; leaves of bulrush and rice cut-grass; seeds of dotted smartweed, halberdleaf tearthumb, arrowleaf tearthumb, bur reed, water parsnip, silky dogwood, and wild cherry.

Another activity on the marsh that I participated in with much interest in the late 1950s and early 1960s, was the banding of some 10,000 red-winged blackbirds. The Patuxent marsh banding program was part of a study of the distribution and migration of the redwing in eastern North America, in which several of us from the Patuxent Wildlife Research Center were engaged. Large traps, 20 by 40 feet (Fig. 8), and Japanese mist nets were used for this purpose. Mist netting was the more productive method. The mist nets were about 40 feet in length and 10 feet in height, and were strung between two steel poles (Fig. 9).

Fig. 9. Don Fankhauser, U.S. Fish and Wildlife Service biologist, at mist net banding station on the Patuxent River marsh. Red-winged blackbirds were intercepted by Japanese mist nets which were placed along roost flightlines. Ten thousand redwings were banded on the Patuxent marsh in late summer and early fall from 1958 to 1965. Most of them wintered in eastern North Carolina.

Nets were placed along the tidal creeks or guts that run at right angles to the river. In the evening the redwings fly downriver to their roosts crossing the guts and are intercepted by the nets. The finely meshed nets are so inconspicuous that redwings, flying at the usual flight speed of 25–30 miles per hour, often cannot avoid the nets which they do not see until about six feet away from them. Trapping and banding redwings was a late-summer/early-fall operation.

As the food supply diminishes on the marsh and cooler weather comes with the first frosts in early October, most of the redwings, which by that time have completed their molt, and the soras, bobolinks, blue-winged teal, and some of the king rails, depart for the South. Redwings from the Patuxent marsh winter along the South Atlantic Coast, mostly in the Carolinas. Some sora and blue-winged teal go as far south as the West Indies and Mexico; and the bobolinks go all the way to Brazil.

Fig. 10. After the hunting season. Railbird boats tied up at dock in December. Low tide on old wildrice marsh, Patuxent River, Maryland. Wildrice plants deteriorate completely by winter. Compare with photograph of hunting scene taken in September.

The departure of these late-summer/early-fall birds of the wildrice marshes occurs at about the time of the arrival of the vanguard of pintails, mallards and other northern ducks. These larger ducks remain on the marsh until the first few days of the hunting season in November, when most of them are "gunned" off of the Patuxent and seek the broader marshes of the Chesapeake Bay system.

The winter marsh is drab and bleak but some plants, such as cattail, retain much of their life-form, providing cover for a few redwings, king and Virginia rails. However, wild rice deteriorates completely and the wide expanse of the marsh that it covers looks as bare and flat as a pancake (Fig. 10).

On an occasional warm January day I have seen the marsh come alive with the spring song, the *okalee* of the male red-winged blackbird. The "Marsh Dandy," flashing its red epaulets, is usually holding forth from atop a muskrat house or the tip of a trapper's pole that marks the site of a muskrat trap.

Fig. 11. Common or Wilson's snipe, known to hunters of bygone days as jacksnipe. Snipe are common migrants in spring and autumn on the Patuxent River marshes. Photograph by Luther Goldman.

By the month of March, spring migration is on, and great flocks of ducks, geese, blackbirds, some snipe (Fig. 11), and yellowlegs are winging their way northward through the Patuxent River Valley. But it is nearly May before the marsh wakes up, and the first fresh green shoots appear above the shallow waters of the riverbed.

THE KING RAIL

The rails are our most secretive birds. They hide in marshes and fly very little, except during spring and fall migration. They depend on their strong legs and swift movement afoot, and the protective cover of marsh vegetation, to avoid danger.

Fig. 12. A king rail walking. One foot is placed in front of the other, thus there is a single line of tracks.

All species of the family Rallidae which are native to North America occur in the Chesapeake Bay Country—this includes the king, clapper, Virginia, sora, yellow, and black rails; also the common and purple gallinules, and the coot. The purple gallinule is a rare visitor from the South.

13

Marsh hen is the most popular of many local names for the king rail and the clapper rail. In Audubon's time, the king rail was known as the freshwater marsh hen, the clapper, the saltwater marsh hen; and although the ornithological texts would have one believe that the king is associated only with fresh marsh and the clapper with salt marsh, there are nevertheless brackish marshes along the lower reaches of certain rivers where both species sometimes occur.

Fig. 13. Note paths made by muskrats in Olney three-square marsh along the Blackwater River in Dorchester County, Maryland. Rails use these pathways while moving through the marsh.

This chapter is concerned with the king rail (Fig. 12); and in the Chesapeake Bay Country the distribution of this species coincides pretty closely with that of the muskrat. Muskrats play an important role in the economy of the rail's life. They create optimum habitat for rails by opening up marshes and producing a network of pathways (Fig. 13) leading to plunge holes. When the tide goes out, water is trapped in the holes and the rails use them as drinking places. Muskrat trails also are favorite places for crayfish burrows. Crayfish are prime food of the larger rails and are usually carried to the tops of muskrat houses for dismantling and eating.

One winter when the Patuxent River was frozen over, I was walking along the edge of the marsh and noticed a king rail feeding in the runway leading to a muskrat den in a bank. This bit of unfrozen runway was only about two feet long and six or eight inches wide, and about the only place the rail could find a little open water.

The muskrat's prime habitat in our tidewater country is an Olney three-square marsh. *Scirpus olneyi,* as it is technically known, forms extensive pure stands in the Blackwater country of Dorchester County, along sections of the Nanticoke, and in yet other slightly brackish situations in tidewater. In one such Olney three-square marsh across the Nanticoke from Vienna, the king rail is quite common. Plants of the rose mallow or hibiscus were sprinkled throughout this marsh at the time when I was making a nesting survey of the rail in June 1965. All nests that I located were at the base of hibiscus plants and none were in three-square. The life-form of the hibiscus with its cradlelike base and broad leaves forming a protective cover or canopy above, makes it well suited for a nesting site; whereas the three-square, which is relatively short and stands erect like so many lead pencils, does not form a very dense cover for nesting.

One of the strangest habitats where I have found king rails is in the Fresh Bay Marsh Community north of Savannah Lake, Elliott Island, Dorchester County. At this station, rails occur where the switchgrass marsh extends inland for a mile or so forming an understory beneath a loblolly pine forest (Fig. 14). The short-billed marsh wren was found in this same pine-switchgrass association. Switch grass, which attains a height of about five feet, retains its life-form throughout the year, thus affording excellent cover, especially in winter when several other marsh plants have deteriorated.

The highest density of king rail populations is found where there is an abundance of crustaceans, a favorite food. When I worked in the Arkansas and Louisiana rice fields 20 years ago, I noticed that king rails were abundant, obviously due to concentrations of crayfish (crawfish or crawdad) in this man-made marsh. I found similar high densities of rails in the brackish marshes at Taylor's Gut, near the Smyrna River in Delaware, where the red-jointed fiddler crab is so abundant.

Once crayfish, fiddler crabs, clams, and larger insects have been ingested, those parts that are not digested are regurgitated in the form of pellets (Fig. 15). Measurements of several pellets examined averaged 2.0 centimeters long by 1.5 centimeters wide. A favorite deposition site is the top of a muskrat house or a raft of debris lodged in the marsh. I have counted as many as 14 pellets on a single muskrat house.

Fig. 14. Habitat of king rail in loblolly pine-switchgrass association, Elliott Island marsh, Dorchester County, Maryland, August 1967. Rails occur on the wet ground, short-billed marsh wrens in the switch grass, and brown-headed nuthatches in the scattered pines. Photograph by Luther Goldman.

In addition to crustaceans, aquatic insects, fish, frogs, grasshoppers, the seeds of aquatic plants also have a high palatability rating with the king rail. Some unusual food items found in gizzards include cherry seeds, skunk hair, feathers and vertebrae of a female red-winged blackbird (probably found dead), king rail eggshell fragments, a small water snake, a mouse, a shrew, fall armyworms, black gum seeds, acorns, and pine seeds.

There is considerable variation in food items taken by different individuals in the same habitat at the same time. Two birds caught in muskrat traps in a tidal marsh on the Choptank River near Dover Bridge, in February 1961, present an interesting contrast. Bird "A" fed entirely on fish, while bird "B" ate a wide and rather unusual assortment of foods, including the seeds of arrow-arum, hackberry, halberd-

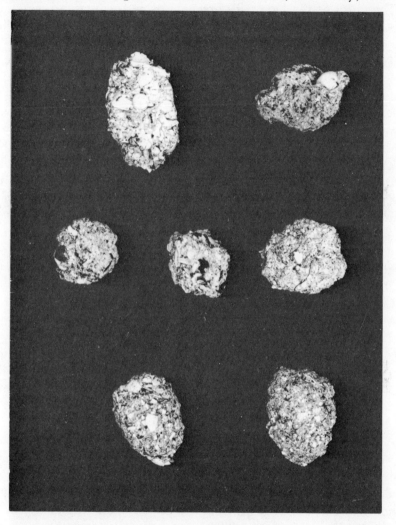

Fig. 15. Exoskeletal remains of crustaceans in regurgitated pellets of marsh hens. Pellets averaged 2.0 cm in length by 1.5 cm in width. Photograph by Frederick C. Schmid.

leaf tearthumb, dogwood, and grape. Bird "B" had also eaten crayfish and a snail. The seeds of arrow-arum contain calcium oxalate crystals and apparently are rejected by virtually all water birds except the wood duck. This was the only time I encountered these seeds during my studies of rail foods.

Such foods as crustaceans also are used by the male king rail in the courtship ritual.

The onset of the king rail's breeding or nesting season is announced by the mating call and in the Chesapeake Bay Country is heard during the first warm days of April.

The *kik-kik-kik-kik* courtship call of the rail and *okalee* of the red-winged blackbird were the two sounds of spring in the Patuxent marshes that I best remember. This courtship call of the courting king rail reminded the pioneers of the Illinois and Iowa prairies of a wagon driver urging on a team of horses, and thus called the bird the "stage driver."

The purpose of the courtship call is for the male to identify with a territory (later used for nesting), and to attract a mate. One male that I had under constant observation for a long period of time gave the courtship call continuously for 18 minutes.

A part of the courtship procedure of the male is a display of its white undertail coverts. Almost always while walking, the tail is cocked or uplifted and the white undertail coverts are extended. While flashing its white undertail coverts, the rail usually flicks its tail up and down.

Courtship feeding, a type of symbolic display that aids in maintaining the pair bond, was observed during the courtship, egg-laying, and incubation periods. In some fresh nontidal marshes, the crayfish was the only food that I ever saw presented to a female during the ritual. In certain brackish tidal marshes, the fiddler crab was used for this purpose. The male usually brings the food item to the female, but sometimes he may stand where he catches the crustacean, holding it in his bill until the female approaches and takes possession.

A mated pair of rails that I observed for a number of days on their breeding territory would descend at low tide from the marsh to a pool in the bed of a tidal creek. The female would usually stand in the pool while the male hunted food for her. He would frequently run up the winding creek bed for 25 yards or so, catch a fiddler crab, and run back to present it to the female. Why he often traveled such distances when there were plenty of fiddlers nearby is not known.

During a two-hour period of observation in an Arkansas rice field, I saw the male of a pair catch seven crayfish, five of which he presented to his mate.

In the Chesapeake Bay Country most king rails nest in May and June. However, a brood of chicks and their parents seen by the writer near

Fig. 16. Nest and eggs of king rail in soft-rush marsh. Note canopy over top of nest.

Fig. 17. Dome or canopy of king rail nest made of spike rush.

the Blackwater River, Dorchester County, on May 8, 1974, is evidence that some king rails begin nesting in March. The incubation period is 21–22 days.

The nest site (Figs. 16–18) is chosen by the male; and on two occasions I have seen a male initiate nest building. The nest may be close to the previous year's nest site. An incubating bird that I banded

Fig. 18. King rail on nest in cattail marsh.

on its nest near the Patuxent River, July 3, 1965, was recaptured in a trap with a brood of eight young on July 8, 1966, 50 feet from the 1965 banding site.

The height of the nest above the water in a marsh usually depends upon the depth of the water. Nests placed two or three inches above the surface of the water may be elevated as much as a foot during a heavy rain and when the water is rising.

The king rail lays a large clutch, averaging 10—11 eggs. I have found several clutches of 14 eggs. B.W. Swales (3) found a king rail nest in St. Clair County, Michigan, that contained 17 eggs; nine laid by the king rail, seven by a Virginia rail, and one by a sora.

Incubating birds seldom flush until an intruder is within 10 feet or less of the nest. As the hatching date approaches, they become even more tenacious. On several occasions I was able to band incubating birds, but not without considerable resistance from them. On one occa-

Fig. 19. Distraction display of king rail near nest. This display is characterized by feigning injury and emitting distress call.

sion when I approached a nest at hatching time, the bird flew from the nest and struck me in the chest. On other occasions they have struck at my legs or have run to my feet where they remained with wings outstretched, pecking away. Often they perform a distraction display by feigning injury as they attempt to lead the intruder away from the nest (Fig. 19).

The newly hatched rail is like a baby barnyard chick or duckling as it is able to leave the nest within an hour or so after hatching. The baby chick is covered with black down that has a faint greenish sheen. The bill has a pied pattern (Fig. 20).

I observed that rail chicks took food from their parents' beaks the first day, and attempted to forage a little for themselves by the second day.

By the time they are half grown they are still accepting food from their parents as well as hunting for themselves. An interesting example of this dual feeding activity was observed at Taylor's Gut, Delaware, in July 1959. An adult king rail and three young approximately five to six weeks of age were observed feeding on small clams *(Macoma balthica)* at low tide in the bed of the gut. The adult bird dug in the mud for the

Fig. 20. Banding a young marsh hen or king rail.

clams, usually inserting its entire head beneath the surface. It would eat four or five clams and then carry one to the young. The clams were swallowed whole. Sometimes one of the young, standing next to its parent, would watch the digging operation and then start digging for itself. At other times, a raccoon came to the spot and dug many clams.

By midsummer, rails are well into the molting cycle. Adult rails drop their wing and tail feathers simultaneously, like ducks and geese, and are thus flightless for about a month. By the first of September, when the railbird hunting season begins, most of the king rails are flying again. However, it should be emphasized that there are still a few flight-less birds about.

From banding recoveries we know that some king rails are migratory. Also, when I lived at Stuttgart, Arkansas, and Alexandria, Louisiana, I heard them calling late at night as they flew over my house, heading northward during the spring migration period. And, there are records of king rails striking lighthouse beacons along the coast and appearing in odd places, such as city streets, during periods of migration.

Winter records for the Middle Atlantic States suggest the possibility of permanent residency by some individuals. In the Chesapeake Bay region there are two records of king rails banded in August at Cove Point and recovered in the same marsh the following January. Also, a six-week-old chick banded July 12, 1968, at the Patuxent Wildlife Research Center, at Laurel, was recovered December 12, 1968, at the same place.

During extended freezes or when there is snow cover, water for drinking is obtained by ingesting snow or small chunks of ice. I saw a bird swallowing a chunk of ice three inches in length by a half inch in width.

Captive king and clapper rails that I kept in a cage at the edge of a pond at the Patuxent Wildlife Research Center preferred to rest on the ice rather than in a more protected section of the cage provided with a windbreak and bedding of straw. During alternating periods of freezing and thawing, spherical chunks of ice, up to the size of a baseball, stuck to the tails of the clapper rails (the salt-marsh species), and smaller particles stuck to their breasts. Strangely, particles of ice virtually never adhered to any part of the plumage of the king rails.

In the Chesapeake Bay Country, king rails make it through the winter best in brackish tidal river marshes, where the tidal action and partly saline water keep the marsh open most of the time.

BALD EAGLE LORE

The bald eagle, once a common bird in the Chesapeake Bay Country, is now on the rare and endangered list, and it is a red-letter day when one is sighted. When I began studying bald eagles in the early 1930s, the veteran ornithologists of the tidewater country used to tell me that there was an eagle's nest on an average of every three miles of the Chesapeake shoreline. Jackson M. Abbott (4) who conducts a bald eagle nesting survey each spring in the Chesapeake Bay area, reported the

Fig. 21. Charlie Rittler at eagle nest, Gunpowder Neck, Harford County, Maryland, March 1936.

1973 eagle population of Tidewater Maryland and Virginia at about 66 pairs with active nests. In that year, 24 of the 66 nests produced 41 eaglets.

In the early 1900s, a favorite activity of the few field ornithologists in Maryland was climbing to eagle nests (Fig. 21). I suppose that it was the great size and height of the nests that lured the egg collectors, banders, and photographers to the eagle's aerie. Egg collecting as a hobby died out in the 1930s, long before the Bay Country eagle population began to decline. In the heyday of the egg collectors, a set of eagle eggs (Fig. 22) sold for ten dollars.

Fig. 22. Bald eagle eggs in nest at Rhode River, Anne Arundel County, Maryland, February 1936.

The bald eagle is one of our earliest nesting birds. A pair near the Blackwater Wildlife Refuge, in Dorchester County, began building a nest in December. The nest, built in a loblolly pine, was in use for most of seven months. The lone eaglet fledged in June. Most nests in the Chesapeake Bay Country are constructed of sticks and cornstalks, and some include chunks of sod. Nests are usually lined with grass.

A pair of eagles will return to the same nest year after year until the nest tree blows down or the birds are otherwise disturbed. Each year they add new material to the nest until some reach mammoth proportions. Professor Herrick of Oberlin College reported in Bent's *Life Histories of North American Birds* (5) that a nest on the south shore of Lake Erie near Vermilion, Ohio, was in use each year for 35 years (but probably not by the same pair of birds). The nest was 12 feet deep and 8½ feet wide at the top. Some nests that have blown down have been dismantled stick by stick and found to weigh as much as two tons.

The average date of egg-laying in the Chesapeake area is about February 28. Two or three eggs comprise a clutch.

On cold winter days with the wind whipping across the Bay, climbing to an eagle's nest at 80 or 90 feet is quite a challenge. I have had such fearless friends as Bruce Overington and Fred Schmid of Laurel, and Charlie Rittler of Baltimore, who would not give a second thought to such feats, and made regular trips to aeries each late winter and early spring for photography and banding purposes. I would not have climbed to some of those nests for a thousand dollars. I climbed to an occasional low one of 60 feet.

One of the problems of the eagle nest climbers was the matter of getting up from under and around the edge of the nest to the top of it, since some of these structures are 6 to 8 feet wide at the top. Once while I was photographing a month-old eaglet (Fig. 23) lowered to the ground for me by Fred Schmid, I took so long posing the eagle for shots that Fred stretched across the six-foot-wide nest and took a nap. Looking up, I could see no part of him.

In some of the more difficult climbs it might take an hour to reach a nest. But the climber could descend from that same nest in two or three minutes. The equipment used by most climbers was that of the telephone pole lineman. The method of returning to earth was to have a long rope, one end of which was thrown over a limb near the nest and tied around the waist of the climber. A man on the ground holding onto the other end of the rope that had been played out 100 feet or so along the ground, walked toward the base of the tree allowing the man at the nest to swing down about as fast as an elevator descends.

Some of the best concentrations of nesting bald eagles in the 1930s were at Aberdeen Proving Grounds and Edgewood Arsenal, near the head of the Bay. These Army bases had extensive land holdings at that time with large parcels not in use; and being near the Bay, they were prime nesting territories for eagles. I remember the highest eagle's nest that I saw in Maryland was on Spesutie Island, which lay a short distance offshore from the Proving Grounds, in the Susquehanna Flats. Dick Harlow, the former football coach at Western Maryland and Harvard whose hobby was ornithology, told me where the nest was located. The nest was 115 feet above the ground in a huge white oak. To reach Spesutie one afternoon, Charlie Rittler and I crossed over on rotten ice that rocked up and down as we inched our way toward the Island. We were so scared that we stayed about 50 feet apart and had a rope tied to each other in case one of us fell in. The return trip was even more hazardous as darkness had overtaken us.

Fig. 23. Young bald eagle removed from nest for photographing, Morgantown, Charles County, Maryland, April 1961.

One of the questions people used to ask me about those eagle nest climbing expeditions concerned the behavior of the birds as we climbed toward the aerie. They were surprised to learn that the adult eagles spent their time watching us from a perch a hundred yards away or circling high overhead.

Eagles live near the Bay because fish is one of their main foods. They are good fishermen, but much of the fish that they eat is carrion washed up on the shoreline. Sick or wounded waterfowl are another important food in the Bay area, as are muskrats, some of which are taken from traps.

In his studies of muskrats at Blackwater National Wildlife Refuge near Cambridge, Maryland, Frank Smith (6) found evidence of bald eagle predation on this furbearer.

"Muskrat remains were found in approximately half of 62 eagle pellets examined, 44 collected from beneath an occupied nest."

Smith also examined food remains from an eagle nest in use for more than 30 years, that had blown down in a storm. There were 30 muskrat skulls among the nest debris.

Since bald eagles feed to a considerable extent on carrion and disabled animals, it is probable that many of the muskrats taken were not healthy or live animals. Smith presented an interesting example:

"In June 1932 a bald eagle was seen to drive a turkey vulture from the top of a muskrat house where the vulture had been eating something. The house was a considerable distance from the observer, and by the time he reached it, the eagle, which in the meantime had been eating, had flown away. Bone fragments of a partly grown muskrat were found. Had only the eagle been seen, it might have been held responsible for the killing, but as the observer saw the eagle drive the vulture from the food, the muskrat must have been dead even before the vulture found it."

In the 1930s and '40s, when I was taking pictures of eagle nests (Fig. 24) and their contents in the Chesapeake Bay region, I recall seeing a muskrat trap on the rim of several of the nests. Certainly the traps were not taken from the marsh as nest-building material.

A few years ago Fred Schmid and I came upon an eagle on the beach below the Calvert Cliffs feeding on a dead diamondback terrapin—gourmet's delight! At a nest Fred climbed to near Morgantown, on the Potomac, he found the remains of a coot and a grebe, two ducklike birds.

The Blackwater section of Dorchester County, Maryland, has always been good bald eagle country, and especially so since 11,000 acres of it have become a national wildlife refuge. Today it is one of the last strongholds of the eagle in the Chesapeake Bay region.

At the present time, Blackwater has the densest breeding population of bald eagles in the Chesapeake Bay Country of Maryland and Virginia. Jackson M. Abbott (7) reported seven nesting pairs in an area with a diameter of about ten miles in this section of Dorchester County, in 1971.

As already indicated, the future of the bald eagle in the Chesapeake Bay Country is not bright, nor is it so in two other former strongholds,

Florida and the Great Lakes region. Only in Alaska, where there is less pollution and disturbance by man, is the bald eagle still common.

Shooting, pesticides, and human encroachment at nesting sites are the major causes of the decline of the population. Shooting has probably been the major factor. Although eagles are on the list of protected birds, in the more remote areas where they occur, some people do not hesitate to shoot them; and some youngsters who have .22 rifles do not even know that they are protected. Nearly half of the dead eagles sent to the Patuxent Wildlife Research Center for pesticide residue analysis and other studies, have been shot (8).

Fig. 24. Bald eagle and nest, Black Walnut Creek, Anne Arundel County, Maryland, March 1936.

Lethal levels of pesticides have been found in the brains of eagles. Pesticides also are the cause of eggshell thinning and consequent breaking of eggs or sterility.

One may wonder if the bald eagle will survive much longer in today's world of the Chesapeake Bay Country. Sometimes all it takes is an outboard motorboat driving up and down a creek near the shoreline site of an active eagle's nest to cause a desertion and another nesting failure for that season.

FROM A BLIND ON THE GUNPOWDER MARSH

The blind in this case is not a duck blind, but a photographic blind.

In the mid-1930s I used to gather my gear, which included a large Graflex camera, a tripod, a canvas blind, and a pup tent for camping out, board a train in Baltimore and head for the Gunpowder River marsh. The marsh is located about 15 miles northeast of Baltimore in an area that used to be referred to as the "Necks." The "Necks" are a series of peninsulas separating Back, Middle, Gunpowder, Bush, and the Susquehanna Rivers, all on the Western Shore of the upper Chesapeake Bay.

In the old days, prior to World War II, the Gunpowder was a fairly good ducking and railbird shooting marsh, having an abundance of submerged aquatic plants that attracted the canvasback and widgeon, and the wild rice on which the sora fattened. Due to silting in of the marsh and pollution, these choice foods no longer occur in profusion. The predominant aquatic vegetation in those days as at present, was cattail.

Of all of the emergent aquatic plants, the cattail is probably the best nesting substrate for such marsh dwellers as the red-winged blackbird, long-billed marsh wren, common gallinule, and least bittern. All four species were common nesting birds in the days of my photographic expeditions on the Gunpowder.

The best time to photograph these birds was at the height of their nesting season, in late May and early June. The blind was erected within six or eight feet of the nest. During the process of installing the blind that close to a nest the tenant was frightened away, but once the blind was set up and I was inside, it was not too long before the bird returned to incubate the eggs or brood the young.

Sitting in a blind on a hot June day in an open marsh is no fun unless something interesting is happening at the nest upon which your camera is focused. Usually it was so steaming hot that I was stripped down to my drawers. Of course, it is always exciting when the bird returns to the nest, settles down, and the light is just right for making a picture; and often events of interest occurred while I was looking through the peephole of a photographic blind, even when the bird was away from the nest.

With some species, both sexes take turns at incubating or brooding the newly hatched young. Where only the female incubates or broods, the nest is left unattended for short periods when she leaves to feed or for whatever other purpose. I do not recall now whether both sexes of the least bittern (Fig. 25) participated in nest care. In a definitive study that I made in Arkansas of the little blue heron, both sexes incubated; and as the least bittern is in the same family, both sexes of that species

Fig. 25. Least bittern at nest in cattails. Gunpowder River marsh, June 1936.

probably do also. However, when one least bittern at a Gunpowder marsh nest left and there was no immediate changeover or replacement, the unattended eggs were visited by a long-billed marsh wren that immediately pipped four of the six eggs. The wren was not interested in the contents of the eggs. Perhaps it was the nesting bittern's intrusion in the wren's breeding territory that motivated the wren.

At another active least bittern nest that was unattended for a period, a Baltimore oriole pipped one of the eggs of the clutch. Orioles do not nest in the marsh but in sycamore trees that border the Gunpowder.

A bird of special interest to me on the Gunpowder marsh in the mid-1930s was the common gallinule (Fig. 26). In those days it was known as the Florida gallinule; but in 1957, the American Ornithologists' Union Check-List Committee, arbiter of such matters, changed the name to common. The common gallinule belongs to the rail family, closely resembling the coot, another member of the Rallidae.

Fig. 26. Adult Florida or common gallinules in cattail marsh. They occur in fresh and brackish marshes in the Chesapeake Bay area. This member of the rail family was a common nesting species in the Gunpowder River marsh in the 1930s. Photograph by Luther Goldman, U.S. Fish and Wildlife Service.

The Gunpowder marsh is one of the few places in the Chesapeake Bay Country where I have found this species to be a common nesting bird. Stewart and Robbins (9) in *Birds of Maryland and the District of Columbia* reported the distribution of the common gallinule in the Chesapeake Bay Country as follows: "Breeding: Fairly common in the marshes along the Gunpowder River estuary (Baltimore and Harford Counties); uncommon and local in tidewater areas of the southern half of Dorchester County; possibly breeds sparingly in other tidewater areas. . . ." In recent years it has been found to be fairly common near Dames Quarter, in Somerset County.

I found seven nests on the Gunpowder marsh in 1936—three on June 14th, three on June 21st, and one on July 4th. Nests were usually fashioned from pieces of cattail, and most of the nests were in little islands or atolls of cattail growth. Clutches numbered six or seven eggs.

Fig. 27. Nest of hatching Florida or common gallinule eggs at Gunpowder River marsh, July 4, 1936.

On one occasion I was sitting in my blind about 10 feet from a gallinule's nest as the eggs were hatching (Fig. 27). I thought it unusual to see the adult in attendance (sexes are alike) pick up a piece of one of the eggshells and eat it. I found out some years later that this was not unusual for some birds, but was probably the exception rather than the rule. I saw a king rail that had a nest in an Arkansas rice field do the same. But in most king rail and purple gallinule nests that I examined in Arkansas and Louisiana, bits of the hatched eggshell fragments had filtered down toward the bottom of the nest. In food habits studies where I was examining stomach contents of birds in the laboratory, occasionally I would find fragments of eggshells of birds of the same species. Most songbirds remove the eggshells from the nests. It seems to be some of the larger birds that eat the shells or just let them break up into bits and remain in the nest, particularly the precocial type where the young leave the nest within an hour or so after hatching.

Fig. 28. Long-billed marsh wren about to enter nest at Gunpowder River marsh.

One of the two most abundant nesting songbirds of the Gunpowder cattail marsh is the long-billed marsh wren (Fig. 28). The other is the red-winged blackbird. I was especially interested in gathering some information on the nesting behavior of the longbill.

This wren builds a globular-shaped nest that looks something like a coconut standing on end; and the male builds numerous dummy nests within the breeding territory.

The male longbill arrives on the nesting ground a week or so before the female. It sets up a well-defined territory which it defends mainly by song, and occasionally by chase, and proceeds to build from two or three to a dozen dummy nests. The dummy nests, scattered throughout the territory, are similar in size and shape to the female brood nest, but are not as well constructed. The inner chamber is not lined with the rail, bittern or duck feathers that form the soft bedding for the eggs in the female's nest.

Most of the dummy nests are built a few days before the females arrive, and ornithologist A.C. Bent (10) suggests that this activity of the territorial males gives the birds an outlet for surplus energy until the females appear.

The nesting season of the marsh wren is a long one, extending from early May to late August. All of the Gunpowder marsh nests that I found were placed in cattails, three or four feet above the water. While I was observing marsh wren nesting behavior from a blind during several hours in mid-August, a sora, a Virginia rail and a shoveler (duck) passed beneath the nest, but were not challenged by either wren parent.

Longbills are hardy birds as some of them occur in the Gunpowder marsh through the fall and winter. However, the tagging of a series of these birds with numbered metal leg bands would probably show that the resident nesting wrens migrate south for the winter and are replaced by birds that have moved in from more northern marshes.

THE REEDBIRD

The reedbird, ricebird or bobolink (Fig. 29), as it has been variously known, has always been one of my favorites. There are many reasons why, but the ones that come to mind at the moment have to do with its association with wildrice marshes, one of our most attractive wetland areas; its identification with domestic rice culture in the South Carolina Low Country in years gone by, a romantic era in a romantic section of the country; and because the plaintive *pink* of the reedbird high in the sky over the late summer marsh is one of the early sounds of southward-bound birds that tells the ornithologist that the exciting event of fall migration will soon be gathering momentum.

Bobolink is the standard common or book name for this species, and the one that is usually applied to birds on the nesting ground. Reedbird was the Chesapeake marsh gunner's name 75 years ago when the reedys, as they were also known, were gunned on the Spring Garden Flats of south Baltimore along the Patapsco or along the Patuxent near Upper Marlboro. Ricebird was the commonly used term for the species in the Carolina Low Country because of its depredations on domestic rice. Indeed, ricebird was its first name, the one applied by Mark Catesby, the father of North American ornithology.

Its penchant for rice was suggestive to the scientific ornithologists who gave it the name *Dolichonyx oryzivorus,* which translated means long-clawed eater of rice. *Oryza* is the technical term for domestic rice.

The male bobolink has two plumages. In the spring its plumage is mostly black and white; after the postnuptial molt in summer, its plumage is yellow, closely resembling the female, which is much the same in appearance at all seasons. The male also has a prenuptial molt which gives it its spring breeding plumage.

In the spring the reedbird or bobolink nests in meadows well north and west of the Chesapeake Bay Country. The nesting locale in Maryland is the Alleghany Plateau of Garrett County, in the extreme western part of the State. North of Chesapeake Bay, the nearest nesting birds are in central-eastern Pennsylvania. The nesting range in the east extends into the Maritime Provinces of Canada.

In the southward flight, beginning in late summer, reedbirds are more coastal in distribution, with the main route of travel in the East through the Delaware Valley and Chesapeake Bay Country. Major concentra-

Fig. 29. Reedbird or bobolink perched on wildrice plant. In late summer migrating reedbirds flock to the wildrice beds of our fresh tidal river marshes. Illustration by John W. Taylor.

tions occur in fresh and brackish tidal river marshes where they feed on wild rice, millet, and other aquatic plant seeds, and where they roost at night. Many of them leave the marshes during the day to feed on the seeds of foxtail grass that grows in and around the edges of almost all Maryland and Virginia cornfields.

The earliest arrivals from the North that I saw in 1974 were at the head of the Bay in the vicinity of the Susquehanna Flats, on July 22nd.

The late summer flight begins to build up by the last two weeks in August with a peak being reached during the first two weeks in September. I do not believe that there is much migration at night during the fall, at least not at this latitude. The period of heaviest migration appears to be during the two hours after dawn, with some movement throughout the day into late evening. The fact that they form roosts, as do blackbirds in our marshes in fall, supports my belief, since blackbirds are diurnal migrants.

In the old days, reedbirds, being in good requisition for the table, were much sought after by hunters. This was in the late 1800s and early 1900s. Like all birds that migrate, they accumulate a considerable amount of fat to sustain them on the long journey. Since they are among those of our migrants which travel the longest distance, they are among the fattest birds on the southward flight, with fat deposition averaging about 25 percent of body weight.

My old Baltimore naturalist friend, Percy Blogg, who hunted reedbirds before I was born, has written an interesting account of gunning these birds. His article, entitled "Bobolink (Reedbird)," appeared in the *Rally Sheet* (11), monthly publication of the League of Maryland Sportsmen.

"To a certain element of Maryland gunners *opening day* on the marshes was looked forward to with as much anticipation as *opening day* on the celebrated Susquehanna Flats.

"It was the first of September that the law permitted the shooting of reedbirds on the Patapsco flats, Patuxent, Gunpowder and other marshes. Before daybreak enthusiastic gunners with their 'outfits' could be seen taking their places along the edges of wild-oat [wildrice] fields previous to the time the birds began their flight toward favorite feeding grounds. The outfit of the reed bird hunter was most varied: boats of all descriptions, but all of shallow draft so as to be able to get through the numerous 'guts' and shallows which make up great and picturesque marshes.

"The birds were generally shot as they 'traded' to and fro over little channels or 'guts' that intersect the marsh, and it was very necessary to shoot them at such a time that they would fall into the open water. Their plumage at that season harmonized so perfectly with the foliage of the oats that it was hard to find them unless they were 'marked' very carefully.

"The market gunner hunted differently as with him birds were money and he generally waded through the marsh seeking the best feeding places, where he could fire into a flock as they sat on the reeds, thus getting several at one shot. Just before the shot he gave a little *whoop* to notify anyone who might be among the reeds that he was going to fire, and you could sometimes hear a half dozen answering *whoops* coming across the marsh. In this way he could locate the other gunners and not shoot toward them.

"The Patapsco flats were once one of the best feeding grounds in the state, and the extent of the oat field increased each year. About 1910 the oats extended beyond the old Long Bridge which crossed the river east of the present Hanover Street structure and one had only to get a Curtis Bay car and ride over the bridge through the tallest of the oats to see hundreds of reed birds and blackbirds feeding close by. The proximity of this marsh to the city made it very popular and, while there were plenty of birds, there were also scores of hunters. The Patuxent, Gunpowder and other marshes were not so accessible in those days when automobiles were not available. Then, too, the B&O Railroad to Curtis Bay ran directly across the marsh and, whenever a train came through, the birds would rise in great clouds, making excellent shooting for an hour or more until they settled again among the oat fields."

The piece of land at the south end of Hanover Street Bridge is known to this day as Reed Bird Island; and nearby is Reedbird Avenue.

Percy Blogg told me that some reedbirds were so fat that when they were shot and fell, their skin would burst open upon hitting the ground.

We are, of course, thankful that the days of hunting the reedbird are behind us and that the shooting of these birds in the Middle Atlantic States wildrice marshes and South Atlantic Coastal domestic rice fields did not decimate their population.

Reedbirds or bobolinks are abundant through our area today during spring and fall migration. An ornithologist friend of mine, Richard Rowlett, recently saw a fall roost of some 65,000 of these birds near Ocean City, Maryland. On September 21, 1960, I estimated the roosting reedbird population on the Bohemia River marsh in the upper Bay region, at 100,000 birds; and on September 10, 1974, I watched some 20,000 reedbirds going to roost in the Nanticoke River marsh near Vienna, Maryland.

I have done some mist netting of reedbirds on the Patuxent marshes for banding purposes; and for the same reason in sorghum fields near the river. I placed nets between rows of sorghum and caught and banded 250 in one field in early September. One of the birds from this operation was later recovered in Quebec.

Although in the same family (Icteridae) as the blackbirds, they stay to themselves, rarely mixing with the redwings, grackles, cowbirds or other blackbirds that often feed together in the same habitats. This same habit of segregation usually prevails at the marsh roosting site which, however, may be in the same section of marsh with the blackbirds, but usually several hundred feet apart.

Most of the reedbirds of the Chesapeake Bay's tidal river marshes have moved southward by late September, but we do have a scattering of birds lingering until early October. My friend Walter Harmer of the old Butler Island rice plantation at Darien, Georgia, near the coast, writes me that he usually sees the first reedbirds (ricebirds in that area) by September 10th.

The main flight to the wintering ground is down the Florida peninsula, across to Cuba, on to Jamaica, and then a long flight across the Caribbean Sea to South America. Most of them winter in Brazil and Argentina. The spring flight northward is somewhat the same, with the exception being a rather strong spur flight across the Gulf of Mexico to the lower Mississippi Valley and northward.

One of the most impressive ornithological sights that I have witnessed was a tremendous reedbird migration through south-central Florida one early May at nightfall. I was standing at the head of Lake Okeechobee on a gusty evening when beginning just before dusk, continuous strings of reedbirds or bobolinks flew by, below 100 feet altitude, for nearly two hours. There was no question that several hundred thousand birds of this species were on the flight.

My association with this remarkable bird has been a long and frequent one; and each fall when I hear the *pink* of the reedbird, it stirs memories of those days in the early 1930s, when as a boy I would drift in a rowboat down a tidal gut through the Patuxent marsh at dawn on a misty morning, with reedbirds breaking from their roost and descending all about me to feed on the succulent wildrice seed.

THE ELLIOTT ISLAND BLACK RAILS

The little black rail (Fig. 30) is the most secretive bird in North America. One of the best places for the bird watcher to *hear* one is at Elliott Island in Maryland's Chesapeake Bay Country. Elliott lies between Fishing Bay and the Nanticoke River, and is mostly salt and brackish marsh.

Fig. 30. Adult black rail, approximately life-size, captured by hand at midnight at Elliott Island, Dorchester County, Maryland, June 1958.

This diminutive rail, about the size of a sparrow, lives in the vast salt-marsh meadow or savanna (Fig. 31), a short-grass marsh studded with still-water ponds or potholes (Fig. 32). It travels about inconspicuously in the marsh grass, and rarely flies during the day; apparently it is more active at night for its call is heard almost exclusively then; and it performs extensive nocturnal migrations between wintering grounds and breeding grounds.

As far as we know, black rails occur at Elliott Island only during the summer-half of the year. They arrive in late April and are gone by September or October. The period of calling extends from the court-ship through the nesting season; i.e., from the last week in April until the middle of July.

In summer the black rail shares the Elliott Island salt-marsh meadow with the black duck, blue-winged teal, willet, red-winged blackbird, seaside and sharp-tailed sparrows, muskrat, meadow vole, and diamond-back terrapin.

Fig. 31. Salt-marsh meadow, summer home of black rail at Elliott Island, Maryland, May 1959. Vegetation is salt-meadow cordgrass, Olney three-square, and loblolly pine.

The salt-marsh meadow is not flooded by normal high tides, but is soggy most of the time. It has a firm bottom, enabling farmers in some sections to harvest the salt-marsh hay, as the salt grass and salt-meadow cordgrass is locally known.

So dense is the windswept and matted-down meadow that to move about in it, black rails often have to use the tunneled runways of the meadow mouse or vole. Most black rails call at night from small shallow depressions in the marsh meadow that are covered sparsely with a broadleaved type of cordgrass (*Spartina alterniflora* or *S. cynosuroides*).

They are very rarely seen during the day; and only on a cloudy day have I heard one occasionally call very briefly.

Ornithologists or birders come to Elliott Island late at night to listen for black rails. They begin calling at between 9:00 and 10:00 p.m., and continue until just before dawn. Sometimes a birder can stand in one spot and hear a half dozen calling. The best place to hear them at Elliott is in the vicinity of Pokata Creek, along the road to the village of Elliott.

For years ornithologists did not know the call of the black rail. They heard several unknown calls at night in Elliott Island marshes inhabi-

Fig. 32. Still-water pond in brackish bay marsh, Elliott Island, Maryland, May 1959. Pond is the result of a muskrat "eatout."

tated by rails, but no one seemed to be able to determine whether they were hearing the black, yellow, or the courtship call of the Virginia rail. After much perseverance, by stalking several calling rails and collecting them, they were not only able to identify the calling birds as black rails, but to determine which sex gave which call. I participated in some of these nocturnal expeditions.

On a June night in 1958, at about midnight, Robert E. Stewart, John S. Webb and I tried a technique where the three of us walked abreast as we stalked a calling bird; the man in the middle had a shotgun, and the one on each side held a flashlight. When a rail began calling from a position of 20 or 30 feet in front of us, the men holding the flashlights crossed the beams or triangulated on the spot from which the calling appeared to come. Then the man in the center would shoot at the spot where the beams crossed. But a minute or so after each shot, the bird would start calling to our side or behind us. After a half dozen unsuccessful attempts at shooting the bird, I attempted to stalk it and capture it by hand. Each time the bird called, I approached the spot and often came within three or four feet, when it stopped calling and moved a few yards away. Finally, after a period of about five minutes of not hearing it, it began calling close to me, and as I pointed my flashlight downward in the short marsh grass, I could see it standing and calling right between my feet! It was a very exciting moment as I reached down and grabbed the little black rail. Later successful captures were made with Japanese mist nets, various types of traps, and by catching by hand when a bird was lured to a black rail tape-recorded call.

What is thought to be the territorial or primary advertising call or song of the male black rail may be described as *ki-ki-kerr;* and we are reasonably sure that the *kree-e* call is given by the female. Both sexes have a number of different, less audible calls or notes in their repertoire. I have heard at least six of them. The black rail that I caught that June night was kept in captivity for two years, and shown to over a hundred persons. During the entire time in captivity the only sound it made was *er!*

To find a black rail is difficult; to find its nest is even more so. John Weske, a graduate student from Cornell University working on a master's thesis project, spent nearly five months during the nesting season studying the black rail's ecology, and did not find a single nest. Nests are placed on the ground and are hidden beneath the salt-marsh hay. An endeavor to find one is like looking for the proverbial needle in a haystack.

Weske was in the black rail's habitat day and night and lived in a house belonging to a duck club right out in the salt-marsh meadow where he could hear black rails calling from any room in the house. He spent much of his time looking for nests and enlisted the help of many of his friends in the search. He even brought in a dog that was especially trained for locating wild duck nests, but to no avail. The dense, uniform cover of the extensive salt-marsh meadow makes it virtually impossible to locate a nest at Elliott Island. In other parts of the country where the black rail occurs in more varied habitat, the nests are occasionally found. Only two nests have been found in Maryland. Both were located in Dorchester County and were found accidentally.

Black rails are occasionally heard in a few other Chesapeake Bay marshes. Late at night in June 1958, I heard three at Dames Quarter, in Somerset County. Other persons have since heard them there. Charlie Handley, a mammologist at the U.S. National Museum, caught one in a mousetrap at Chincoteague; and in June 1974, Hal Wieranga, with the use of a tape-recorded black rail call was able on several occasions to lure an adult and two small chicks to the edge of a marsh at Sandy Point. This was the first time black rail chicks had been seen in Maryland.

Notes on the Color of the Black Rail's Legs *The Artists' Perpetuation of an Error*

John James Audubon, the pioneer ornithologist-artist, called the black rail the "Least Water Rail." He did not know the bird in life, but had been given specimens in 1836 by one of his Philadelphia naturalist friends, Titian Peale.

Audubon's painting of one of these specimens in his *Birds of America* (12) shows the bird with yellowish-green legs and feet! Yet, the feet are grayish. How could he have erred? And how could all of the great bird artists, Fuertes, Peterson, Singer and others that followed Audubon, perpetuate the error? Still, nearly 150 years later, the two most popular field guides still show the legs and feet of the black rail as yellowish-green. Robert E. Stewart, my colleague in the U.S. Fish and Wildlife Service, and I corrected this error in a paper published in the *Auk* (13), technical journal of the American Ornithologists' Union; and John Weske, who handled at least 14 live specimens in the field, corroborated our findings; but the bird artists are still making the error for which Audubon was originally responsible.

SPRING ON A RED-WINGED BLACKBIRD MARSH

Spring comes to the bird world before it comes to ours, that is if we associate spring with the northward migration of birds and the onset of the nesting season. By mid-January in the Chesapeake Bay Country, two of our largest birds, the great horned owl and the bald eagle, have started nesting; in February, some birds that have been wintering with us and some that have wintered to the south, have started moving northward. By March, northward migration is in full swing all the way from the tropics to Canada, and local birds such as the barred owl, woodcock, mourning dove, horned lark, and some others, are nesting.

Banding studies have shown that most of our wintering red-winged blackbirds are birds that summer to the north of us, in New Jersey, New York, New England, and eastern Canada. With the onset of northward migration, several million redwings are still wintering on the Eastern Shore, and somewhat fewer west of the Bay, waiting for the ice to break up on New England ponds. At the same time, the first local or native redwings are beginning to arrive, returning from a winter in the Carolinas to the same nesting marshes they left the previous summer.

The marsh comes alive with their return, and with the spirited *oak-a-lee* of the adult male holding forth from a swinging cattail out in the pond (Fig. 33). Many of these early arriving males return to the same section of the same marsh, and to the same territorial perch from which they oversee their staked-out territory—which is usually a quarter of an acre or less in size. Redwings generally are colonial nesters, though probably not by choice, but because of habitat requirements.

Earliest adult males usually appear on ponds near my home in the Patuxent River Valley by the second week in February. In the ensuing month, additional adult males are arriving to stake out territories, and by the middle of March the marshy pond has reached its carrying capacity.

Some adult territorial males are displaced by later arriving males, but we know that some of the birds that stake out a territory in mid-February are still holding the same territory as late as early August. This we found out from banding and color-marking. A territorial male that was marked at a Kent Island, Maryland, marsh on February 27 was still holding territory on August 8! This bird was marked four different ways by Tom Crebbs, a Virginia Polytechnic Institute graduate student that I was instructing in ornithology. We called the bird "four-way." Tom placed a colored plastic collar around its neck, a metal numbered band on one leg, a colored plastic band on the other, and painted its tail white. The bird soon lost the neck collar. In numerous trips to its territory throughout the spring and early summer, we always found the

Fig. 33. A displaying male red-winged blackbird. From a painting by L.A. Fuertes, courtesy U.S. Fish and Wildlife Service.

bird at hand. The white tail would be replaced by a new black one in the late summer molt.

It is indeed interesting that some male redwings return to their territories so early in the year, since the females (Fig. 34) do not enter the territories for mating until April, and nest building seldom begins before May 1. But because of the competition for optimum territories, males must return much earlier than females in order to stake out and defend prime nesting areas in a marsh. Early in the breeding season, the adult males do not spend the entire day on territory. Small groups of them may spend considerable time foraging in nearby fallow agricultural fields or in some other section on the marsh. On extremely cold days in late February and early March, they may be absent from the marsh for most of the day, and their song is heard only early in the morning and late in the evening.

Territories are held or "defended" through song, displays, chasing, and bluffing. A male generally uses threats and displays in border encounters with other males rather than resorting to combat. As long as a male is active on a territory, his boundaries are usually respected. Ownership of a piece of marsh is signaled by what is known as the "song-spread" of a male on its territorial perch or toward the end of a short flight over its territory. As the song is given, the red shoulder patch, or epaulets, are prominently displayed and are erected and often vibrated, and the wings and tail spread. The song-spread may be given by a male when another male approaches the border of its territory, and as a part of the courtship display when the females arrive on the marsh. Territorial males are much more aggressive toward other redwings than toward other species of birds, except for species such as grackles and blue jays that rob nests.

A territorial male is usually polygamous and has one to three mates which nest within its territory. The number depends upon the extent of optimum nesting cover. Both adult and immature or yearling females may be a part of the harem. According to Wright and Wright (14), the immature or yearling male apparently is capable of reproduction, but is driven out of optimum nesting areas by the more aggressive adult males.

By April, females that have been in the vicinity of the marshes for several weeks, begin looking over territories for optimum nesting conditions. Prime nesting territories must have plants that will support and hide nests, and are near a source of food.

During the period that females are searching out nesting territories, the frequency of displaying or posturing by the males is accelerated. When the female settles in a territory, the pair bond has been formed and there is much sexual chasing, which is a part of the courtship ritual but does not end in copulation. The male seldom comes in contact with the female during the sexual chase. The chasing occurs during the early

Fig. 34. Female red-winged blackbird perched on soft-rush plants. Photograph by Luther Goldman.

part of the mating period and ceases when the period of copulation occurs. Copulation only occurs when the female gives the signal, which she does by posturing or display.

Females are restricted to the mate's breeding or nesting territory by the aggressive action of males holding adjacent territories, except when

Fig. 35. Nest and eggs of the red-winged blackbird.

the female chooses to fly a considerable distance beyond the nesting colony to some foraging area. At first a female is antagonistic toward any other female that enters her mate's territory as a part of his harem, but as nesting begins, she is less concerned and then defends only a small area about her nest.

The courtship period, which extends from pair formation when the female settles in the territory, to egg-laying, may last two or three weeks. In the Chesapeake Bay Country, nest building begins about the first of May. John Webb and I examined 650 active redwing nests in tidal marshes and found that 78 percent were located in high-tide bush and groundsel bush, marsh shrubs of nearly identical life-form. After the nest is built, the three or four eggs (Fig. 35) are laid on consecutive days. Incubation is about 12 days, and the nestlings are in the nest for a similar period. The female, only, is concerned with nest building, incubation, and feeding of nestlings. During this period the male is still busy defending his territory by singing and displaying, and occasionally chasing an intruding male. Females are very persistent in their efforts to reproduce. If nests or nest contents are destroyed by predators or storms, there may be two or three renesting attempts. Also, in the middle and southern latitudes, redwings may have a second brood following a successful first attempt.

In examining hundreds of nests in the course of a nesting season, I have observed that toward the latter part of June and in July, some females lay eggs that are much smaller than normal size, and are infertile. One such egg was the size of a hummingbird's egg, or less than one-fifth normal size.

By the fourth of July, nesting is over for most redwings and adult males are beginning to desert their territories. But there are always a few females that are hanging on and attempting to raise a brood in August. I have found an occasional active nest with eggs as late as the third week in August and a female feeding recently-fledged young in the first week in September. Thus in some areas, the prenesting and nesting season of the red-winged blackbird extends from the second week in February, when the very earliest males establish nesting territories, until early September when the very latest fledglings are still being attended by females. I suppose this is one of the reasons that the red-winged blackbird is probably the most abundant bird in North America.

OSPREYS OF THE ESTUARIES

The Chesapeake Bay is the largest estuary in the United States. It is of special interest that this largest estuary supports the largest breeding osprey population in the country. The size of the bay area, its twisted shoreline, the dendritic pattern of its river system, and its bountiful fisheries have contributed to this favorable status. There were approximately 1,450 nesting pairs of ospreys in the entire Chesapeake Bay system in 1973. This estimate is based on aerial surveys made by Henny, Smith, and Stotts, as reported in *Chesapeake Science* (15).

The lower reaches of our tidal rivers are the main fishing grounds of the ospreys. Each spring they return to these estuaries on St. Patrick's Day (so the watermen tell us) to look over old nesting sites or find new ones on duck blinds, channel markers, dead trees or on the chimney of a deserted house near the water. They choose other man-made and natural sites and in more remote areas, such as uninhabited islands, may even build on the ground.

Fish hawks (or fishing hawks, as they are more popularly known and more appropriately called) spend about six months of their life in the Chesapeake Bay Country. Most of them do appear on or about St. Patrick's Day, and most have left the Bay Country by October.

They travel a considerable distance to and from the wintering grounds. From banding recoveries we find that most of Chesapeake Bay's ospreys winter in Brazil, Colombia, and Venezuela. One bird was recovered as far south as Argentina. A nestling banded at Turkey Point, Cecil County, July 2, 1954, was recovered in Brazil on September 25, 1954.

The osprey is important to the waterman and anyone interested in the natural resources of the Bay Country. The local people look forward to the return of this harbinger of spring, and are entertained by its spectacular dive into the water.

The usual method of fishing is to soar over an area, often at several hundred feet, until it spots a likely prey, then it hovers over the spot to get a bead on the fish and at the opportune moment, with wings half folded, plummets downward with a force that sometimes carries it beneath the surface. Shortly after emerging, when taking off, it gives a shake of its body to rid itself of water. Once a fish is grasped in both feet, the legs are positioned so that one foot is in front of the other and the fish is held parallel to the body of the bird with head directed forward. A smaller fish may be held in one foot.

Another method of fishing is for the bird to fly close to the surface with one or both feet dragging through the water. This disturbance will cause the fish to jump. Also, occasionally ospreys feed on dead fish found on the beach or floating in the water.

It may seem out of character that the osprey sometimes should feed on animals other than fish. J.W. Wiley and F.E. Lohrer, in an article in the *Wilson Bulletin* (16) entitled "Additional records of non-fish prey taken by ospreys," reported that near Tampa, Florida, ospreys were observed capturing cotton rats.

A number of other non-fish items occasionally taken include mice, rabbits, ducks (probably sick or injured), shorebirds, and turtles. The reason for the departure from the normal diet is due to scarcity of fish in the nesting area, or murky water, inclement weather, lack of fishing skill of young birds, and the attraction of easily captured crippled birds.

Most of the osprey's time in the Chesapeake Bay Country is spent fishing and propagating young. Almost immediately upon returning to the breeding grounds, ospreys seek out old nest sites and fishing territories or establish new ones. In the six months that they are in the Bay Country, much of their time during a four-month period is spent repairing nests, incubating eggs, and procuring food for the nestlings.

Henny, Smith, and Stotts (ibid) found in their 1973 survey of nest sites that 31.7 percent of the population was nesting in trees; the remaining birds utilized duck blinds (28.7 percent), channel markers (21.8 percent) and miscellaneous man-made structures (17.8 percent). On Bloodsworth Island, a naval bombing range, Henny *et al* reported that such unique nesting sites used included several car bodies used for bombing targets, an unexploded 1,000-pound bomb, and several radar towers.

Nests, whether placed in trees or on man-made structures (Fig. 36) are constructed of sticks and cornstalks, with the occasional addition of pieces of sod, the carcass of a seagull, an old tennis shoe, part of a life preserver, broken oar or some other odd item. When windrows of dead eelgrass, a submerged aquatic plant, are available along the shoreline, this material is used for lining nests (Fig. 37).

Old nests are mended or added to and some used for many years may become massive structures. There are records of nests eight feet in diameter and five feet in height. Some nests have been known to have been occupied for nearly 50 years, but probably not by the same birds. Some of the larger nests may have tenants nesting in the side of the structure, as I have found house sparrows and common grackles using such sites.

The average clutch size is about three eggs. The incubation period is about a month, and the young are in the nest about two months after hatching to the time they fledge or are able to fly. For a number of

Fig. 36. Osprey alighting on nest located near St. Michaels, Talbot County, Maryland, July 5, 1935.

days after fledging they use the nest as home base. The parents will continue to bring food to them until the young can fly well enough to fish for themselves, which they learn to do without instructions.

A favorite of people who live near the water, the osprey is jealously protected and encouraged to nest on their lands. However, in some estuarine areas man's activities, often inadvertently, have resulted in a decline in osprey breeding populations. The Chesapeake Bay population appears to be adjusting to such intrusions and is holding its own.

Unsuccessful reproduction and man's encroachment on its habitat are prime factors in the population decline in most of the U.S. range. Poor reproduction is alleged to be partly due to pollution of the estuarine habitat; and the principal cause of disturbance of nesting sites is

Fig. 37. Young ospreys in nest on abandoned wharf in Chesapeake Bay Country. The nest is lined with eelgrass, a submerged aquatic plant and important food of some waterfowl, particularly brant. Big Annemessex River, Somerset County, Maryland.

due to motorboating in the summer during the critical stages of osprey reproduction. New seashore housing developments and the removal of nests from channel markers by the Coast Guard also are contributing factors.

Because of the tremendous interest in this species and an awareness of a decline in national populations, for the past decade or so ornithologists have been investigating productivity and other aspects of the osprey's life history and ecology in some parts of its range. Jan Reese, an ornithologist operating out of St. Michaels and Tilghman's Island, Maryland, has been the principal investigator of ospreys in the upper Chesapeake Bay area; and Mitchell Byrd, of William and Mary College, has been conducting similar studies in the Virginia part of the Bay.

Reese's studies over a period of nearly 15 years are probably the most intensive ever made of the osprey. His principal study areas are the estuaries bordering the Talbot County shoreline on the Eastern Shore of Maryland. Each year he censuses and determines the productivity of osprey populations in that area, and has additionally contributed to the cause of conservation by constructing many artificial platforms for nests, which substantially increased osprey production in Talbot County waters. Between 1964 and 1969, he installed 133 nest platforms, 81 of which were used.

Reese's investigations, as reported in the *Auk* (17), journal of the American Ornithologists' Union, have shown that the Talbot County osprey population is still producing at levels close to those prevailing before 1960, and well above those of most other U.S. populations. As stated in his latest published report in *Maryland Birdlife* (18), Reese found 1973 productivity to be the best in the past decade. In his study of 114 nests, he found 163 large young, for an average of 1.43 fledglings per active accessible nest. Henny and Wight's life table, published in the *Auk* (19), and based on banding and recovery data for New York and New Jersey ospreys from 1929 to 1947, shows that each adult female must produce between 0.95 and 1.30 immatures each year to insure population stability.

In most sections of the Bay, the nesting osprey population is probably at the same level as it was 100 years ago. Frank Kirkwood surveyed an area in Queen Annes and Kent Counties for osprey nests in 1892; and Jan Reese went over the same area 75 years later (1968). Their figures for distribution and size of the breeding populations were remarkably similar (20).

BLACKWATER

Blackwater is the name of a dark-colored river that winds through the vast tidal marshes of Dorchester County on Maryland's Eastern Shore. The Blackwater flows from three swamps lying at the head of the marsh. These swamps, Gum, Kentuck, and Moneystump, apparently are the reason for the dark-colored water of the river. Farther south on the Coastal Plain, almost all waters flowing from swamps are dark.

Fig. 38. Canada geese leaving marshes at Blackwater National Wildlife Refuge, Dorchester County, Maryland, to feed in nearby corn-stubble fields. Photograph by Luther Goldman, courtesy U.S. Fish and Wildlife Service.

Dorchester County's marshes are the most extensive of any in the Chesapeake Bay system; and those through which the Blackwater flows go by the same name as the River. The whole complex, located a few miles south of the town of Cambridge, is simply known as "Blackwater." A part of the scene, and so characteristic of the area, are the loblolly pines that border the marshes. The loblolly, essentially a southern pine, reaches its northern limit a little farther up the Delmarva Peninsula.

Some 11,000 acres of this country lie within the Blackwater National Wildlife Refuge, an important link in the chain of migratory waterfowl refuges along the Atlantic Flyway extending from Canada into Florida. Blackwater is a good all-around waterfowl area; but it is best known today for its large wintering Canada goose population that spreads out to loaf and feed in Refuge marshes during much of the day, and moves out in spectacular formations often around sunset to forage in nearby corn-stubble fields (Fig. 38).

Fig. 39. Salt-marsh meadow. Vegetation is mostly salt-meadow cordgrass and salt grass. Summer habitat of black rail, black duck, blue-winged teal, seaside sparrow, muskrat, meadow vole, and diamondback terrapin.

Dorchester's marshes and all others in the Chesapeake Bay system are typed mainly on the basis of location, size, salinity, and plant associations. The marshes of southern Dorchester County in the Blackwater area are known as the Brackish Estuarine Bay type. Such marshes are located near or are influenced by large bodies of salt water. The Blackwater River drains into one such body, Fishing Bay. Broad salt-marsh meadows (Fig. 39) are a characteristic feature of this marsh type. These marshy meadows, which are flooded only during exceptionally high tides are dominated by salt-meadow cordgrass and salt grass.

Olney three-square or three-cornered grass (Fig. 40), a prime muskrat and goose food, is the dominant plant in extensive, poorly drained shallow depressions of the marsh that often are covered with surface water. Olney three-square is one of the dominant types at Blackwater Refuge. Narrowleaf cattail occupies much the same zone as three-

Fig. 40. A stand of Olney three-square at the Blackwater National Wildlife Refuge, Dorchester County, Maryland. Plants in this stand average about one foot in height. Rootstocks and stems of three-square are an important food of the Canada goose.

square, and the dominance of one or the other in an area is usually a matter of which one gets the head start.

Muskrats are abundant at Blackwater for the same reason they are numerous in Louisiana's brackish marshes—extensive stands of Olney three-square. Three-square mostly grows in peaty soil, another requirement for a good muskrat marsh. In a bottom of peaty humus a muskrat can make tunnels and canals with firm sides. This is hardly possible where the bottom is sand or mud. Muskrats enlarge ponds and create new ones, and so improve waterfowl habitat.

In my travels around Blackwater and other Chesapeake Bay marshes, I found that wherever muskrats are trapped, king, Virginia, and sora rails become casualties since they use the runways or trails where the traps are placed. Whenever I have encountered muskrat trappers, I either have seen king rails removed from traps or have been told of the many that are caught incidental to muskrat trapping. One trapper that I know caught 50 king rails during the course of a two and one-half month's trapping season.

While making a study of muskrat in Blackwater marshes from 1949 to 1952, my friend and colleague in the Department of the Interior, Van T. Harris, made some interesting incidental observations of ecological relationships of meadow voles (mice) and rice rats in tidal marshes (21). Dr. Harris concluded that fluctuating water levels in tidal marshes, as compared with nontidal marshes and wet meadows, must impose additional problems on vole and rice rat populations. He found that voles and rice rats lived in both occupied and unoccupied muskrat houses.

"By living in muskrat structures, mice gain protection from weather and tides. They use old muskrat leads in their movements through the marsh and probably profit from bits of food left by muskrats. No advantage to the muskrat is suggested by this relationship. The circumstantial evidence from mouse trapping at occupied and unoccupied muskrat houses would indicate that neither muskrat or mouse was directly harmed by common occupancy of muskrat houses. If the presence of muskrats were detrimental to mice, the mice would be found more frequently in unoccupied houses."

Both rice rats and meadow voles were occasionally trapped at the same muskrat house.

Black ducks (Fig. 41), like muskrats, have long been a hallmark of Blackwater country. At Blackwater, as in other black duck production areas of the Eastern Shore, blacks not only nest in marshes (Fig. 42), but choose a variety of sites for depositing their clutch of eggs. Vern Stotts and David Davis, who conducted a nesting study of the black duck in the Chesapeake Bay Country in the period 1953-1958, reported in *Chesapeake Science* (22) that this species nested in marshes, upland fields and woods, on duck blinds, and occasionally in old nests in trees. About 19 percent were on duck blinds, and 70 percent of these were on the roofs of the blinds. Three hens laid their eggs in deserted great blue heron nests that were 70—90 feet above the ground in pines.

Unlike the black duck, which is found nesting throughout most of Chesapeake Tidewater, the nesting blue-winged teal (Fig. 43) population of the Bay area is found mostly in Dorchester and Somerset Counties, Maryland. It was not known to ornithologists as a nesting bird of Bay marshes until about 1930 when Talbot Denmead, an ornithologist with the U.S. Biological Survey, saw an adult and brood in the course of a canoe trip he made down the Blackwater River. A year later, Oliver Austin, Jr., also of the Biological Survey, found nests and eggs of this species in the same area. Of course, the native hunters and trappers knew about the nesting of the teal in Blackwater marshes long before the ornithologists.

Fig. 41. Banding a young black duck.

The bluewing nests mainly in the salt-marsh meadows (Figs. 44 & 45), and spends the summer feeding in the little pothole ponds that result from muskrat "eatout" activity.

With the approach of autumn, most of Blackwater's native blue-winged teal migrate to the West Indies and beyond. Several bluewings banded in Maryland were recovered in winter in the Bahamas, Cuba, Puerto Rico, and the northeastern coast of South America.

As the blue-winged teal leave Blackwater in early autumn, the van-guard of waterfowl from the northern "duck factory" appear in the local marshes. By the end of fall migration, thousands of Canada geese and ducks have arrived in this section of Dorchester County where most of them spend the winter.

Fig. 42. Nest and eggs of black duck in big cordgrass beside tidal gut, Dorchester County, Maryland, May 1959.

Of special interest are the geese. Banding studies have shown that most of them have come from breeding grounds in the James Bay

Fig. 43. Blue-winged teal (drake), one of three species of ducks that nest in the brackish marshes of Dorchester and Somerset Counties, Maryland. Others are the black, and less commonly, the gadwall. Photograph by Dave McLauchlin, courtesy U.S. Fish and Wildlife Service.

region, just south of Hudson Bay. In the early 1940s, the wintering population of Canada geese at Blackwater National Wildlife Refuge seldom numbered more than 5,000 birds. Today, 30 years later, the population ranges between 50,000 and 100,000. The marked increase in the population has been due primarily to the building of additional freshwater ponds that not only provide resting areas, but also natural food; farming operations on the Refuge that produce corn, millet, wheat, soybeans, and other crops; and the residue corn left from the mechanical harvesting operation on farms surrounding the Refuge.

Fig. 44. Incomplete clutch of eggs of blue-winged teal. Nest will not be lined with down until clutch is complete and incubation starts. Elliott Island, Maryland, May.

People who own land around the Refuge have exceptional goose shooting. Geese follow a routine of working back and forth from the Refuge to nearby stubble fields. They are hunted mostly from blinds and pits dug into the stubble fields. An unusual method practiced by a few hunters is to shoot from platforms placed high in trees, as the geese skim the tops of the woods when moving from the Refuge to surrounding croplands.

The variety of waterfowl at Blackwater is only a part of its rich bird fauna. For this reason, the Refuge was selected as a locality for one of the annual Christmas Bird Counts sponsored by the National Audubon Society. The Blackwater Count, made by volunteer bird watchers, has been conducted annually for the past 26 years. The count or census area is a 15-mile circle that includes most of Blackwater Wildlife Refuge, a part of Fishing Bay, and a part of Elliott Island. The count is made on a single day during the period December 21–January 1. Over 100 species are recorded on that single day each year. The discovery of

Fig. 45. Nest of blue-winged teal in salt-marsh meadow *(Spartina patens* and *Distichlis spicata)* near Savannah Lake, Dorchester County, Maryland, June 2, 1961.

13 long-eared owls was the highlight of the 1974 Christmas Count. Chan Robbins heard five near the Bestpitch bridge. I have observed 30 species of waterfowl in a week's time during the winter in southern Dorchester County.

Blackwater marshes are particularly favorable for rails, shorebirds, egrets, and herons. Virginia and king rails are numerous throughout the year, occurring mostly in narrowleaf cattail and three-square marsh types; and where there is a mixture of herbaceous marsh plants and woody shrubs. The Gum Swamp section, adjacent to State highway 335

Fig. 46. Woodcock on nest at Blackwater National Wildlife Refuge, near Cambridge, Maryland. Photograph by P.J. Van Huizen.

and about a mile or so south of the Blackwater River bridge, is one of the best areas in the State for king rails. I have seen them there regularly for the past 20 years. The habitat is composed of a mixture of narrowleaf cattail, soft rush, switch grass, swamp rose, several shrubs, and in some sections a scattering of loblolly pines.

Clapper rails occur in the saltier cordgrass and needlerush marshes bordering Fishing Bay. Some work their way up the Blackwater River into the brackish marshes.

Migrating shorebirds forage for invertebrates in the open mud flats and shallow pools of the salt-marsh meadow and three-square marsh. On May 8, 1974, I counted over 100 each of greater and lesser yellowlegs, and some 500 dunlins or red-backed sandpipers.

The woodcock, a member of the shorebird family that is usually associated with wet thickets bordering marshes, is a common spring and fall migrant at Blackwater, and occasionally nests there. Peter J. Van Huizen, the Refuge's first manager, found a woodcock nesting in the piney woods near the marshes in the 1930s (Fig. 46).

Because of the protection afforded by the Refuge and the extensive area of swamps, marshlands, tidal creeks, rivers, and bays in southern Dorchester County, the Blackwater section is the principal concentration area of bald eagles in the Chesapeake Bay system. According to Bill Julian, manager of the Refuge in the early 1970s, 15 or 20 bald eagles and two or three golden eagles usually winter in the area; and six or seven balds nest there each year.

Blackwater is a unique area, and is one of the best for wildlife on the Eastern Shore inland from the Atlantic Coast of Maryland. Where else can you stand in one spot next to a cattail marsh listening to the mating call of the seldom-seen king rail; at the same time looking at seven rare endemic Delmarva fox squirrels feeding along the edge of a woods bordering the marsh, and with a slight turn of the head focus your eyes on a pair of bald eagles perched above their nest? This I did on May 8, 1974.

THE CHINCOTEAGUE SALT MARSH

The Atlantic Coastal salt marshes are the last frontier of the eastern United States. They remain as the largest parcel of land that has changed the least, and exist today as they have ever since their substrate emerged from the sea and became a series of salt marshes decked with cordgrass.

Man has been chipping away at the salt marshes for the past 100 years, filling in and gouging out; but extensive undisturbed areas still exist. In fact, about 2,000,000 acres stretch from the Maine coast to Key West.

The coastal salt marshes lie between the barrier islands that front on the ocean and the mainland. They either border the lagoons or bays behind the offshore barrier, or fill up most of the in-between area with their solid stands of salt-marsh cordgrass and mosaic of channels and guts through which the tidal waters pass.

This vibrant natural community has been briefly but aptly described by my ornithologist friend, Ivan R. Tomkins, in his book, *The Birdlife of the Savannah River Delta* (23):

"The salt marsh is more than an expanse of cordgrass and black rush. It is a wide expanse of soft wet earths laid over by a skin of grass roots. It is creek edges that are under water at high tides, but strips of mud flats when the tide drops. It has pools entrapped, filled with tidal water or rain water. It is perforated with the holes of fiddler crabs, burrowing shrimp, and marine worms. The grasses have periwinkles [snails] attached to their stalks, and when there is dew the whole marsh is a-shimmer with the webs of countless spiders. When the tide comes among the grasses the grasshoppers casually swim from place to place. The marsh changes from hour to hour and from day to day. This day there will be a neap tide that scarcely touches the grass stems, another day the whole marsh is under water for a time; and when it recedes, the turbulent flow carries sediments from the marsh table down into the creeks."

The Atlantic Coastal salt marshes that I know best are at Chincoteague, Virginia (Fig. 47). The marshes surround the island of Chincoteague, which is separated by a channel from Assateague, the barrier island along that section of the coast (Fig. 48).

Chincoteague, because of its protected inside location, has been inhabited by fishermen, oystermen, and the like for over 100 years, while Assateague has until recently remained a wild barrier beach with a scattering of loblolly pines, and wild ponies that swam ashore several hundred years ago from a shipwrecked Spanish galleon.

Chincoteague is one of the most important concentration areas for birds along the Atlantic Flyway, and its physical features combining offshore waters, ocean beach, barrier island woods, lagoons, mud flats, and salt marshes attract a formidable aggregation of migratory birds. Some 250 species have been reported from the area.

Fig. 47. Salt marsh at Chincoteague. Note laughing gull on post.

The salt marshes, with their extensive pure stands of cordgrass, tidal pools, guts, and mud flats, are a principal focal point of this array of birds. The cordgrass marshes are the center of production of the molluscs, crustaceans, and aquatic insects upon which the shorebirds, rails, herons and egrets, laughing gulls (Fig. 49), boat-tailed grackles, and seaside sparrows feed. The cordgrass marsh also is the principal cover type for the secretive marsh hen or clapper rail which hides and builds its nest there.

Fig. 48. Assateague Light on the barrier island across the channel from Chincoteague. Foreground shows marshy habitat of clapper rail, black rail, and seaside sparrow.

The 40 or so species of shorebirds—the sandpipers, plovers, curlews, and others (Fig. 50) that forage along the tidal flats and shallow marshy pools—are mostly passage birds that in late summer are en route from the nesting grounds in the arctic tundra to wintering grounds in the West Indies and South America. The stopover during the spring flight northward is of shorter duration as the shorebirds have a limited time to reach the breeding grounds at that season.

Fig. 49. The laughing gull is one of four species of gulls that occur regularly in the Chesapeake Bay-Chincoteague area. It is a native bird that nests on marshy islands in the bays or lagoons behind the ocean barrier beach. Photograph by Luther Goldman, U.S. Fish and Wildlife Service.

The willet (Fig. 51) is the local shorebird of the Chincoteague salt marsh. Its cries, *pul-wil-willet*, the *chac-chac-chac-chac* of the clapper rail, the laughing gull's complaining high-pitched cries, and the eerie song of the seaside sparrow, are the sounds that one identifies most with the salt marsh.

But the marsh hen or clapper rail (Fig. 52) is the best known bird and best typifies the avifauna of the salt marsh. This gamebird spends its entire life there, where it feeds principally on the fiddler crabs which are caught when the receding tide exposes the bordering mud flats. Marsh hens are generally quiet at high tide, but as the tide recedes, their discordant *cac-cac-cac* or *chac-chac-chac* can be heard all over the

Fig. 50. Chincoteague is one of the important concentration areas for migrating shorebirds along the Atlantic Coast. Two of the common shorebirds that stop over for a few days while en route to the breeding or wintering grounds are the dowitcher (left) and the knot.

marsh. As one bird begins to sound off, there is a chain reaction as others join in. During the nesting season, in April, May, and June, a new sound is heard on the marsh, the mating call of the male clapper. The *kik-kik-kik* mating call of the clapper and king rails sound identical, and sometimes may be heard continuously for ten minutes.

Most marsh hens build their nests along the edge of the narrow tidal guts that thread their way through the marsh. The cordgrass is taller in this zone where more sediment accumulates and builds a small levee along the bank of the gut.

Fig. 51. The willet is the local shorebird of Chincoteague salt marshes. It gets its name from its call: *pul-wil-willet*. Photograph by Luther Goldman, U.S. Fish and Wildlife Service.

The nest (Fig. 53) is placed but a few inches above the mean high tide level, and has a canopy which conceals the eggs from marauding fish crows, and a ramp for easy access and a quick exodus.

Fig. 52. The clapper rail best typifies the avifauna of the salt marsh. Photograph by Anthony Florio.

Fig. 53. Nest and eggs of clapper rail in salt-marsh cordgrass, Chincoteague, Virginia.

Marsh hens lay large clutches of eggs. This compensates for the loss of so many clutches when spring or flood tides occur during the nesting season and inundate the marsh. The clutch size during first nesting attempts averages nine or ten eggs. Nesting peaks in the latter half of May. Renesting attempts following destruction of initial clutches by high tides or predation by fish crows may continue until early July. Clutches of renesting or second attempts at Chincoteague averaged only five eggs. The nesting density in some sections of marsh is high, and in the early 1960s in just a few acres I found 40 occupied nests in one day.

Fig. 54. Atlantic brant flying by marsh and duck blind at Chincoteague Bay, Virginia. Unlike Canada geese, which they somewhat resemble in appearance and size, brant do not fly in a wedge-shaped formation. Most of the Atlantic brant population winters along the coast from New Jersey to Norfolk.

September 1st marks the opening of the marsh hen hunting season. Hunting is done mostly when there is a "marsh hen tide." Such a tide occurs when a north wind pushes the normal high tide up even higher. Under these conditions a boat can be poled through the marsh grass forcing the birds to flush. Some birds are killed along the edges of creeks at low tide when they come out of the marsh grass to feed on the mud flats. This form of hunting is known as "mudding."

September is also the time when most Chincoteague marsh hens begin their departure for the wintering grounds located along South Atlantic Coastal marshes from southeastern North Carolina to northeastern Florida.

According to Robert E. Stewart (24) who, with an assist from John H. Buckalew and Gorman M. Bond, banded over a thousand of these birds at Chincoteague in 1950 and 1951, some clapper rails waste little

Fig. 55. Greater snow geese over Chincoteague, Virginia. Most of the greater snow goose population winters along the Virginia coast. Photograph by Luther Goldman; Bureau of Sport Fisheries and Wildlife.

time in traveling from their breeding grounds to the wintering area. This is indicated by one immature bird that was banded at Chincoteague on August 26, 1950, and recovered in northeastern Florida on September 24, 1950. Other evidence that some of the rails migrate early is furnished by the record of one banded at Chincoteague on August 15, 1950, and recovered about 60 miles to the south on September 6, 1950. Another banded at Chincoteague on July 28, 1951, was recovered in South Carolina on September 16, 1951. A few marsh hens winter at Chincoteague; some of them have migrated from their summer home in New Jersey coastal salt marshes.

Because its winters are not so harsh, and because of its protected lagoons and extensive salt marshes, Chincoteague is an important wintering area for waterfowl, including the Atlantic brant (Fig. 54) and the greater snow goose (Fig. 55). Virtually the entire population of those two species winters along the Atlantic Coast from southern New Jersey to the Virginia-North Carolina line. In the fall, brant and snow geese

Fig. 56. Brant in the shallows at Chincoteague. Principal food of the brant at this site is sea lettuce *(Ulva)* an alga.

migrate to Chincoteague from their nesting grounds on the islands of the Arctic Sea.

In recent years the total population of greater snow geese has not numbered higher than 50,000 birds—a considerably smaller figure than that of the wintering population of the lesser snow goose of the lower Mississippi Valley, Texas Coast, and California. For a number of years there has been no hunting season on greater snows.

The traditional food of the snow goose on the wintering grounds is the rootstocks of salt-marsh cordgrass. Winter wheat, now planted more extensively in the coastal sections, has become a new food source for them, much to the consternation of the farmer and the conservationist. Wildlife managers will probably keep busy in ensuing winters herding the geese from the winter wheatfields back to the salt marsh.

The Atlantic brant population has fluctuated in the last 50 years from a low of about 20,000 to a high of about 250,000. The low point occurred in 1930, when eelgrass, which had comprised about 80 percent of the brant's diet, disappeared almost entirely due to drought and a disease of the plant. But brant learned to adjust to other foods and made a remarkable comeback. The 1974 population totaled about 100,000 birds.

Brant feed in shallow parts of estuaries (Fig. 56) by "tipping up," much in the manner of dabbling ducks. One of their principal foods now is sea lettuce, an alga. Sea lettuce renders the flesh rather less palatable and for this reason brant are not a favorite of the hunter.

The existence of a series of wildlife refuges and nature sanctuaries from the New Jersey coast into eastern North Carolina pretty well assures the future of the wintering ground for years to come for the greater snow goose and the Atlantic brant. The remoteness of the breeding grounds is favorable to their continued propagation.

NOTES FROM THE NANTICOKE

The Swamp Sparrow

One July day in 1946, Neil Hotchkiss, a U.S. Fish and Wildlife Service biologist, was botanizing in marshes along the Nanticoke River opposite the town of Vienna, when he heard several swamp sparrows singing. This seemed unusual as the swamp sparrow (Fig. 57), a common winter visitor of the Chesapeake Bay Country, was not known to occur during the breeding or nesting season south of western Maryland

Fig. 57. Swamp sparrow, common winter resident but rare nesting bird of Chesapeake Bay marshes. The best known nesting colony is in the Nanticoke River marsh, near Vienna, Maryland. Illustration by John W. Taylor.

and southeastern Pennsylvania. Neil made a note of this event and the following year, his friends, Fish and Wildlife Service ornithologists Chandler Robbins and Robert E. Stewart, visited the area during the nesting season and confirmed his findings.

Because the Nanticoke breeding birds were considerably south of what was thought to be the normal breeding range of the species, Gorman Bond of the U.S. National Museum and Bob Stewart, suspecting that the Nanticoke birds were a new geographic race, collected

Fig. 58. Big cordgrass (the tall plant) and arrow-arum bordering tidal gut in Nanticoke River marsh near Vienna, Maryland. This is the only known nesting area of the swamp sparrow on the Eastern Shore.

several specimens in the summer of 1950. When compared with museum specimens of the nearest known race *Melospiza georgiana georgiana,* the Nanticoke birds were found to have a much darker plumage than their northern relatives. This evidence of geographical variation led Bond and Stewart to conclude that the Nanticoke birds were indeed a distinct race or subspecies, and they proposed the name *Melospiza georgiana nigreacens* to indicate this difference. A description of this new subspecies or geographic race was published in the *Wilson Bulletin* of March 1951 (25).

At a later date, small populations were discovered breeding in the Elk River marsh at the head of Chesapeake Bay and also in the Delaware

Fig. 59. Nest and eggs of king rail in Nanticoke River marsh, Vienna, Wicomico County, Maryland, June 10, 1965. Nest is placed at base of hibiscus plant.

Bay marshes. Specimens collected in southern New Jersey show that in that area, *nigrescens* intergrades with *Melospiza georgiana georgiana*.

Most of the Nanticoke swamp sparrows that I have seen or heard occur in a section of the tidal marsh a short distance southeast of the U.S. Highway 50 bridge. In the late 1960s the marsh in this section was composed mostly of big cordgrass (Fig. 58) and a few scattered shrubs including groundsel bush and myrtle. Nests in this marsh are placed close to the ground or the high-water mark, and if a spring tide (excessively high) occurs during the nesting season, most nests are inundated.

Further ornithological explorations in the Bay Country may turn up some more local populations of breeding swamp sparrows, but thus far, only a half dozen or so of these sparrows have been seen in three other Bay marshes during the summer, and these may have been nonbreeding birds that did not migrate north in the spring.

The Marsh Hen

Sharing the Nanticoke marsh with the swamp sparrow is the marsh hen or king rail. The marsh is not salty enough this far upriver for the other large rail, the clapper.

When I was working on the ecology of the king rail in the Nanticoke marsh in 1965, most of these birds seemed to be concentrated in a broad section dominated by Olney three-square. Scattered through the three-square marsh were colorful hibiscus plants. I located 11 nests of the king rail in the marsh on June 10th. Every one had been placed at the base of a hibiscus plant (Fig. 59). Only one contained eggs—no doubt a recently laid clutch. A spring tide had flushed the marsh and rail eggs were sprinkled about where they had settled on rafts of debris.

Nine years later when I visited this marsh in July, there was very little Olney three-square present. In previous years the three-square marsh was maintained by trappers who burned it over each spring to ensure regrowth, as this is the prime muskrat marsh type in the Chesapeake Bay Country. The shorter three-square had been mostly crowded out or succeeded by taller marsh plants including big cordgrass and switch grass, and a dense mixture of more persistent emergent aquatic plants. This change in the vegetative structure of the marsh does not seem to have affected the king rail population, however.

The Red-winged Blackbird

Thousands of red-winged blackbirds use the Nanticoke River as a migratory flyway, and its marshes as a base of operations in late summer and early fall. When I visited the marsh on September 10 and 12, 1974, most of the redwings had bobbed tails, indicating that they were local birds that had not completed their molt. The red-winged blackbirds' post-nuptial molting period covers about two months, August and September. The entire plumage is replaced during the molt, and when the process is completed they begin moving southward. While undergoing the molt in these late summer hot days, redwings spend a lot of time loafing in the marsh. Extensive foraging flights or migrations are not made because of some missing or only partly replaced flight and tail feathers. Fortunately there are always nearby cornfields, and seed production is at its height in the marshes at that time.

Redwings use the Nanticoke River marshes at all seasons of the year. In late fall and winter the population is composed mostly of birds that have come down from New England, New York, and New Jersey.

Sometimes in the winter I see redwings feeding in the pine trees that skirt the river marsh. They extract the seeds from the pine cones that are still hanging on the tree. Interestingly, these pine seed gatherers were usually males only. Perhaps the male is better adapted for this type of feeding activity because of its longer and more slender bill. I have seen both male and female redwings removing seeds from dangling sweet gum balls on trees bordering the tidal marshes.

The Seaside Alder

Such trees as loblolly pine and sweet gum have a wide moisture tolerance, being found on dry upland sites as well as in wet swampy woods bordering marshlands. Accompanying the trees on these swampy sites are various shrubs, some of which extend well out into the marsh and represent the final stages of the silting in of the marsh; i.e., a shrub swamp. One of the important shrubs of this community is the alder. There are two species in this part of the country—common alder *(Alnus serrulata)*, a widely distributed species, and seaside alder *(Alnus maritima)*, an endemic found only on the Delmarva Peninsula, in the counties of Sussex (Delaware) and Dorchester, Wicomico, and Worcester (Maryland). I have found the seaside alder along the upper reaches of the Nanticoke, near the Delaware line, and especially along Marshyhope Creek.

The seaside alder is distinguished from the common alder by the much larger fruits (Fig. 60) and taller growth of the plant, and unlike the common alder, which blooms in the spring, the seaside alder blooms in early autumn.

Phantom of the Swampy Thickets

Among the less common and less known migrants that I see in the Nanticoke River Country each October are the rusty blackbirds (Fig. 61). They usually occur in the alders of the shrub swamp zone that lies between the inner edge of the marsh and the bordering upland woods. They slip into our territory quietly, and then all of a sudden have gone on their way. A few winter in the Chesapeake Bay Country, but most of them travel further south, returning to our swampy thickets again in the spring en route to their nesting grounds in the northern coniferous forests.

Fig. 60. Catkins of the seaside alder *(Alnus maritima)* (top) and the common alder *(Alnus serrulata)*. The seaside alder is a Delmarva endemic, found only in Sussex County, Delaware, and Wicomico, Dorchester and Worcester Counties, Maryland.

The rusty gets its name from its song, which sounds like someone opening a rusty gate, and also because of the rusty edgings of its winter plumage. In its breeding plumage in the spring, the male is black and the female gray. Both have the conspicuous yellow iris of the eye. When they arrive in the Chesapeake area in the autumn, both sexes have acquired a new and more handsome plumage, very much in tune with our October foliage. In this winter plumage, which develops following the summer molt, the tips of the feathers of the back and head are rust-colored, and the feathers of the breast are tipped with an ochraceous or cream-buff.

Fig. 61. A banded rusty blackbird, common spring and fall migrant usually found in swampy woods and thickets.

They move about in small flocks, only occasionally leaving the swampy thickets to join the huge aggregations of grackles, redwings, and cowbirds that glean the open stubble fields.

On the wintering ground in the Deep South, rustys change their habits somewhat, spending some of their time foraging on the ground in pecan groves. Towards the end of winter they become more vociferous and when they return in the spring to forage among the skunk cabbage habitat of the Nanticoke's swampy edges, they are in full song.

A List of Plants

The following is a list of plants recorded September 12, 1974, in the Nanticoke River marsh east of Vienna, Maryland, along U.S. Highway 50:

arrow-arum
arrowhead
black grass
bulrush, salt-marsh
bulrush, soft-stem
butterweed
cattail, broadleaf
cattail, narrowleaf
climbing hempweed
cordgrass, big
cut-grass, rice
groundsel bush
hibiscus, marsh
jewelweed
lobelia
mallow, salt-marsh

millet, Walter
phragmites
pickerelweed
sedge (undetermined)
smartweed, dotted
soft rush
spike rush, dwarf
sweet flag
switch grass
tearthumb, arrowleaf
tearthumb, halberdleaf
three-square, common
three-square, Olney
water hemp, tidemarsh
water parsnip
wool grass

THE RED-COCKADED WOODPECKER
OF THE MARITIME FOREST

The red-cockaded woodpecker is Maryland's rarest native bird. This southern bird has been observed in the State almost exclusively in the maritime loblolly pine forest of the lower Eastern Shore, where it reaches its northern limit as a nesting bird. The only occurrence records in the State are from Dorchester, Worcester, and Prince George's Counties, with only a single record in the last two counties. Until a pair was observed near Bowie, Prince George's County, On May 11, 1974, none had been seen in the State for about 15 years, or since 1959. The two birds seen at Bowie were undoubtedly wanderers beyond their normal range, as they were not observed on subsequent visits to the area.

The red-cockade is unlike other woodpeckers as it occurs only in pine forests, and nests only in mature or overripe pines that are infested with red-heart disease. To reach this stage a tree must be about 70 years old. A nest tree near Golden Hill, Maryland, was 90 years old and forester Charles Stierly discovered some nest trees in Virginia which were 103–104 years old.

A small bird, only slightly larger than the downy woodpecker, the red-cockaded is known by its large white face patch, transverse stripes on its back, and black cap and nape. A small patch of scarlet feathers on each side of the back of the head or above each ear, in the male, is virtually invisible even at close range.

The red-cockade is noisier than other eastern woodpeckers, therefore one is seldom in doubt about its presence. The call note is like that of a fledgling starling. An ornithologist friend of mine, who is a bit deaf, was able to locate these woodpeckers in forests where they were known to occur, by watching for falling pieces of pine bark as red-cockades scaled the trunks of trees in search of insects.

This southern woodpecker was first observed in Maryland in 1932 by Frank Smith. Smith, a biologist working at the Blackwater National Wildlife Refuge, found several nesting pairs in the loblolly pine woods in that area. It was not seen again until the middle 1950s when it was rediscovered in a small tract of mature loblollys in the same Blackwater country, but off the Refuge, near Golden Hill.

On May 30, 1958, Robert E. Stewart and I located an active nest in the mature tract of pines near Golden Hill. As is usual with most

87

red-cockade nest holes, it was facing toward the west. Numerous other nest holes (some old, some possibly new) were found. Old nest holes are used for roosting.

There were about a half dozen pairs of red-cockades in the Golden Hill colony. Such colonies are characteristic probably because of a paucity of nesting habitat and the woodpecker's exacting demands.

Nest holes are easy to spot as they are surrounded by an extensive area of whitish resin (Fig. 62). They are so conspicuous that in the more open stands they can often be spotted at several hundred feet. Most of this whitish area of pitch or resin is beneath the hole and sometimes may extend down the trunk almost to the ground. The exuding resin is of course due to the work of the woodpecker in drilling many small holes into the cambium layer of the pine in the area of the nest hole. Some ornithologists believe this is done for the purpose of discouraging other birds, squirrels, and snakes from entering the nesting cavity.

Pines infected with red-heart fungus *(Fomes pini)* are selected for nesting because the soft or rotted center makes nest excavating easier for the woodpecker. I have found this woodpecker nesting in five species of southern pines.

Most trees in which nests occur usually look as much alive as healthy trees, and the birds will continue to use the trees until they are nearly dead, or until the sap no longer exudes from the bark.

Because of its highly specialized nesting habits, the red-cockade is becoming a rare bird in most parts of its range. The old diseased and dying pines required for nesting are being culled by foresters. Modern forestry practices call for harvesting trees on a 25-30 year cycle for pulp and possibly up to 60 years for pole or saw timber, long before they reach the stage when they could be utilized by the woodpecker. But there is hope for the red-cockade, as the plight of this bird has come to the attention of the conservationist, and measures are being taken to preserve nest trees in some areas. Many of the large commercial lumber interests are cooperating in this venture; and there will probably always be a scattering of mature pines on large southern estates and in sanctuaries where this unusual nesting bird can succeed.

The mature tract of loblolly pines in which Maryland's last known red-cockaded woodpecker nesting colony occurred was mostly destroyed in the late 1960s. The nearest nesting birds now, to my knowledge, are in southeastern Virginia in the vicinity of Wakefield, Suffolk, and Franklin.

The red-cockaded woodpecker shares its piney woods habitat with the pine and yellow-throated warblers, and the brown-headed nuthatch, species which fortunately do not have such exacting nesting requirements.

Fig. 62. Red-cockaded woodpecker at entrance to nest hole in living pine. The white face patch is the best field identification mark. This southern bird reaches its northern limit on the Atlantic Coastal Plain in Dorchester County, Maryland. Photograph by S.A. Grimes.

For further reading about red-cockaded woodpecker ecology I would recommend a paper by C.C. Steirly, entitled "The Red-cockaded Woodpecker in Virginia," that appeared in the Atlantic Naturalist, October-December 1957 (26).

THE CHUCK-WILL'S-WIDOW AND
BROWN-HEADED NUTHATCH

The Eastern Shore of Maryland and the southern part of Delaware are a northern extension of the South Atlantic Coastal Plain. Forests of loblolly pine bedecking the flat terrain are physical features common to many sections of the Coastal Plain of the Carolinas and Georgia. Loblolly pine has been extended northward along the coast by the moderating influence of the Gulf Stream and the sandy Coastal Plain soils.

Fig. 63. Chuck-will's-widow incubating. Nests are on the ground and usually in piney woods; note pine needles. The chuck-will is closely related to the whip-poor-will, but is more southern in distribution. In the eastern part of the U.S., it reaches its northern limit on the Delmarva Peninsula. Photograph by Ivan R. Tomkins.

Coincident with the range of this southern pine is that of two species of southern birds, the chuck-will's-widow (Fig. 63) and the brown-headed nuthatch (Fig. 64). Both species reach their northern limit on the Delmarva Peninsula.

In Maryland, these two species reach their greatest abundance in the more open stands of loblolly pine (Fig. 65) along the margins of tidal marshes in Dorchester, Somerset, and Talbot Counties; in Virginia, they are common in most maritime pine forests of the Eastern Shore and Tidewater. The chuck-will occurs during the summer half of the year, while the brown-headed nuthatch is a permanent resident.

Fig. 64. Brown-headed nuthatch at entrance to nest. Nesting cavities are usually in hollow-tree stubs or fence posts. In the Chesapeake Bay Country, this southern bird is near the northern limit of its range and occurs mainly in the maritime loblolly pine forests that skirt the tidal marshes in parts of the Eastern Shore and southern Maryland. Photograph by Jack Dermid, courtesy of U.S. Fish and Wildlife Service.

The chuck-will's-widow, like its cousin, the whip-poor-will, is named for its call. Because the calls are similar and because the whip-poor-will is better known, the chuck-will often is called whip-poor-will. The chuck's call is four-syllabled: *chuck-will's-wid-ow;* the accent is on the *wid.* The whip's call is a three-syllabled *whip-poor-will;* the middle note

Fig. 65. Mature loblolly pine maritime forest near Golden Hill, Dorchester County, Maryland. Typical habitat of chuck-will's-widow, brown-headed nuthatch, and red-cockaded woodpecker. These three species prefer the more open stands of pine.

is weak, with the first and (especially) the last accented. Sometimes both species call for several minutes without a pause. Such a series of consecutive calls may number in the hundreds.

The chuck-will is about 12 inches in length, the whip-poor-will about 10 inches. Both species are crepuscular, or are abroad at twilight, and their calling can be heard throughout the night into the dawn.

The chuck is more southern in distribution but in some places, particularly in the Upper Coastal Plain of the South, the ranges of these two species overlap. I know of two localities along the Middle Atlantic Coast where both species are common. Near the mouth of the Bay, just south of Norfolk, I heard nine whip-poor-wills and three chuck-will's-widows on a May night. Fred Scott, a Virginia ornithologist, found chucks and whips to be common on the Northern Neck (peninsula between the Potomac and Rappahannock Rivers) (27). He noted some overlap in distribution, but the chucks were more toward the east and near the rivers and the whips in the higher central part of the peninsula. In the Maryland and Virginia Piedmont and Mountain Provinces, only the whip-poor-will occurs.

The chuck-will and whip-poor-will have exceptionally wide mouths. One member of this family that occurs in Australia has the name frog-mouth; thus, these birds are flying insect traps, and so wide are their mouths (especially the larger chuck's) that occasionally they will swallow a small bird such as a warbler, which is a nocturnal migrant.

The chuck-will and whip-poor-will nest on the ground, and their nests are barely shallow depressions. Two eggs comprise a clutch. Two clutches of the chuck that I saw in Dorchester County in June were lying on top of pine needles as if they had been dropped there just before I arrived.

Although the chuck-will's-widow is mainly a bird of the loblolly pine woods, sometimes it is encountered in the deciduous or hardwood forests of the Tidewater area. Not so the brown-headed nuthatch, which is almost exclusively a bird of the piney woods. The brown-headed nuthatch is one of three species of nuthatches that occur in Maryland and Virginia. It is the smallest, but a winter visitor from the north (the red-breasted nuthatch) is only slightly larger. Best known is the white-breasted nuthatch, more of a deciduous forest bird and relatively uncommon on the Eastern Shore. It visits feeding stations about suburban homes of Baltimore, Washington, and elsewhere on the western side of the Bay.

During the winter half of the year, the brown-head, a gregarious bird, often cavorts with an assortment of other birds that include the Carolina chickadee, tufted titmouse, myrtle warbler, pine warbler, ruby and golden-crowned kinglets, and downy woodpecker. They may range as a group all day foraging through the maritime piney woods. The brown-head is usually the noisiest of the group.

Brown-heads nest in old woodpecker holes, natural cavities of dead pine stubs, and in fence posts. Sometimes they dig their own hole in a dead stub. Nesting in the Chesapeake Bay Country begins by the middle of April. At Elliott Island, in Dorchester County, I have found brown-headed nuthatches and flickers, and brown-heads and bluebirds with active nests at the same time in the same dead pine stubs.

My Georgia ornithologist friend, Bob Norris, who made a definitive study of the brown-headed nuthatch, discovered some most amazing facts about its nesting behavior which are published in his monograph on this species (28). Norris found that some nests are attended by three individuals rather than by pairs. The extra individual was always a male. His relationship with the pair was very close. It appeared from Norris' observations that the extra or secondary male was not mated to the female. However, at the nest the secondary male assisted in feeding the female while she incubated or brooded, feeding the nestlings and cleaning the nest. He would help feed the fledged young and would roost in the cavity with the mated pair. Norris suggests that the presence of threesomes at nests is associated with this species' highly gregarious nature. The fact that the third bird has always proved to be a male suggests that in at least some geographic populations of this species, there are more males than females.

It seems unusual that some of the highest counts of brown-headed nuthatches have been made near the northern limit of its range. Perhaps this is due to a concentration of optimum habitat found in the maritime pine forests with scattered trees that skirt and extend into the tidal marshes. Brown-heads do not like dense pine forests. A total of 214 were reported in one day by a group of bird watchers in Dorchester County, December 28, 1953 (29). The two areas where most of these 214 brown-heads were reported are the Blackwater National Wildlife Refuge and the Elliott Island pine-studded marshes.

RARE BIRD OF THE POCOMOKE

If the red-cockaded woodpecker is the rarest native bird in Maryland, then the Swainson's warbler is in second place. The only locality where this warbler is found in the State is in the Pocomoke River Swamp.

Fig. 66. View along the Pocomoke River, near Snow Hill, Maryland. Note bald cypress trees in left foreground. Swainson's warbler occasionally occurs across the river in a swamp forest.

The Pocomoke River is an arm of Chesapeake Bay whose course travels the length of the Eastern Shore of Maryland, from about the Delaware line to Pocomoke Sound near the Virginia line. Both sides of the river from just below Pocomoke City to the Delaware line are bordered by a cypress-gum swamp (Fig. 66), the northernmost of the southern swamps on the Atlantic Coastal Plain. The Swainson's warbler, red-bellied water snake, and such plants as horse sugar and crossvine are some of the southern specialties that reach their northern limit in the Pocomoke.

Swainson's warblers are not numerous in the Swamp but occur there regularly. They consistently occur in a picturesque section of the Swamp just below the Delaware line, in a sanctuary established by a conservation group known as Delaware Wildlands. A second area where one may usually find two or three pairs is located in the river swamp about two miles below Pocomoke City. The next nearest population of these birds is found in the Great Dismal Swamp, a few miles south of Norfolk.

Swainson's warbler is one of the least known birds in North America because of its limited distribution and its habit of spending most of its time on or near the ground in dense swampy thickets. Even when one catches an unobstructed view, it also is difficult to see because the brownish plumage of its back blends so well with the leafy substrate where it does most of its foraging. But sometimes it comes to the edge of a thicket, mounts a perch 10 or 15 feet from the ground and bursts forth in song. This is where the bird watcher may get a glimpse of the phantom of the swamps as it sings its course of songs for a few seconds, or a minute or two. Its song is loud and ringing and one of the finest of any of the warblers.

The Reverend John Bachman, a Charleston, South Carolina, ornithologist, heard the bright clear song along the banks of the Edisto River in the spring of 1832 and collected the first specimen of this species known to science. He presented the specimen to his friend, John James Audubon, who described it and named it in honor of the prominent English ornithologist, William Swainson.

It was very likely the song that lured Joseph Cadbury, a Philadelphia ornithologist, to the edge of a Pocomoke Swamp thicket where he identified the first Swainson's warbler ever reported in Maryland. Since that time, Swainson's warbler has been at the head of the list of desiderata of bird watchers visiting the Pocomoke and other southern swamps.

Swainson's spends nearly six months in the Pocomoke, arriving there usually in the third week of April from its winter home in Jamaica or Yucatan. The males come first, often returning to the same approximately one-acre territory. John Weske banded a Swainson's warbler on a nesting territory in the Pocomoke Swamp in May 1960, and the bird was recovered in a Japanese mist net at virtually the same place the following four seasons by banders David Bridge and Vernon Kleen.

The usual habitat in the Pocomoke is a damp section of the Swamp where there is seldom standing water, and where there is an undergrowth of a mixture of sweet pepper bush and greenbrier with an overstory of mixed swamp hardwoods (mostly black gum, sweet gum, water oak, red maple, and swamp magnolia) and an occasional bald cypress.

A number of other warblers spend the summer in the same sections of the Pocomoke as the Swainson's, but each occupies a different forest niche. The closest associates of the Swainson's (because they are understory birds also) include the prothonotary, hooded, and worm-eating warblers as well as the Louisiana water thrush (also a warbler). The water thrush and the Swainson's do most of their feeding on the ground, but they seldom cross paths, as the water thrush forages mostly in little swampy pools, while the Swainson's prefers the drier leaf litter. The parula and yellow-throated warblers and redstart (also a warbler) live in the trees, each at its own level above the Swainson's warbler niche.

After having observed Swainson's warblers for hundreds of hours, I eventually wrote a monograph about them (30). I once spent an entire day from before dawn until after dark in a Swainson's warbler territory studying all aspects of its singing behavior. Such facts as how much it sang, how often, when it did most of its singing, what motivated singing, etc., were recorded. Swainson's sings from the ground and from a perch in a bush or on a lower branch of a tree.

I have been particularly interested in the nesting behavior of Swainson's warbler. It builds a large bulky nest (Fig. 67) two or three feet from the ground in which it lays three or four white eggs. It is one of only two species of warblers in eastern North America that lay white eggs. The other is the virtually extinct Bachman's warbler which also nests close to the ground. These two species are the rarest warblers in North America, probably because of the vulnerability of the type and location of nests, and of the pure white eggs. The other species of warblers lay speckled eggs and have better concealed and usually smaller nests. Most birds that lay white eggs nest in hollow trees, such as the woodpeckers and owls, or in the tunnel of a bank, like the bank swallow and kingfisher.

I have spent hours within short distances from nests of Swainson's warblers taking notes of the nest building, incubation, and nestling care. On a July day in the heart of the Dismal Swamp, I sat for seven hours at the base of a tree 30 feet from a nest, watching the activity of a pair of Swainson's warblers feeding and otherwise caring for their three-day-old young.

Following the nesting season, the Swainson's warbler undergoes a molt to replace its worn plumage in preparation for its southward migration to the tropics. One of its routes south from the Pocomoke is by

Fig. 67. Swainson's warbler on nest in dense swampy thicket. It is one of Maryland's rarest nesting birds and is found only in the Pocomoke Swamp.

way of Tangier Island, where several birds have been observed in early fall. Tangier is just beyond Pocomoke Sound.

Fred Scott, one of the operators of a birdbanding station each fall at Kiptopeake, near the southern tip of the Eastern Shore of Virginia, caught a Swainson's warbler in a mist net there in September 1973. The bird may well have been one of those observed that summer in the Pocomoke.

THE PLIGHT OF THE CANVASBACK

It is fitting that John James Audubon, our best known ornithologist and bird artist, chose the Chesapeake Bay as the scene for his famous painting of our most prized waterfowl species. The canvasback (Figs. 68 & 69) is more closely identified with the Bay than any other area in its wintering range. Audubon's painting, executed about 1830, shows a small group of canvasbacks in the upper part of the Chesapeake with Baltimore Harbor in the background.

Fig. 68. Male (right) and female canvasback. This longtime favorite of Chesapeake Bay waterfowl hunters has been declining in numbers in recent years. The canvasback hunting season is presently closed in the Bay area. Photograph by Rex G. Schmidt, U.S. Fish and Wildlife Service.

The lordly canvasback is to the epicure the most celebrated of our ducks. It acquires its delectable flavor from the wild celery (*Vallisneria spiralis*) from which it has been given its specific Latin name *Aythya valisineria*. A difference in spelling of the generic name of wild celery and the specific name of the canvasback is the work of the zoological taxonomists. The canvasback's generic name, *Aythya,* is from the Greek aithuia, meaning a water bird.

The canvasback is an expert diver, sometimes descending to 25 feet. The submerged aquatic plants upon which it sometimes feeds grow in relatively shallow depths, whereas the canvasback may have to go deeper for clams, (presently a more important food). When feeding on

Fig. 69. Canvasbacks in trap ready for banding at Persimmon Point, Potomac River, off King George County, Virginia. Photograph by Matthew C. Perry, U.S. Fish and Wildlife Service.

submerged aquatics, it is more of a digger of roots and other subterranean plant parts than the other diving ducks.

On the wintering grounds, the canvasback occurs mostly in brackish and fresh tidal waters. In this respect, it is more of a freshwater duck than the scaup, ruddy, and other divers.

Stewart and Robbins, in *Birds of Maryland and the District of Columbia* (9), briefly described its habitat as known in the middle 1950s:

"Estuarine waters that contain a plentiful aquatic plant growth, including such species as wild celery, sago pondweed and eelgrass; also on inland lakes and ponds. Locally, canvasbacks occur in large numbers in certain bays and estuaries that contain a rich and varied molluscan fauna."

Until a few years ago, the Susquehanna Flats area of the upper Bay region was one of the principal late fall and early winter concentration areas of the canvasback in the Chesapeake Bay Country. On December 7, 1947, Stewart and Robbins estimated that 100,000 canvasbacks were on the Flats; and on December 27, 1952, approximately 91,000 were there. However, because of the disappearance of certain submerged aquatic plant foods, the Flats are no longer an important area for canvasbacks. Deterioration of the submerged flora in some sections of the Bay is due to pollution and siltation or muddying of waters from storms such as hurricane "Agnes" and from farming and construction work on the shores of the Bay. A certain amount of light must penetrate the surface of the water for the growth of submerged aquatics.

A scientific paper published by Stewart, Geis, and Evans in 1958 (31), indicated the status of continental canvasback populations in the early and mid-1950s. From surveys made after the hunting season in January, they estimated that the average wintering population during the period 1952-1956 was approximately 508,000. According to the authors, the largest concentration occurred in the Chesapeake Bay area (maximum estimate of 420,000 in 1954) and accounted for about half of the total continental population.

The canvasback population has had its ups and downs over the years, but recently the story has been one of dramatic decline. In the winter of 1973-74, the estimated population for the Chesapeake Bay was only 60,000 birds; and 205,000 for the Continent. There has been no hunting season on canvasbacks in the Chesapeake Bay area for the past several years.

Because of its great popularity as a table delicacy, its challenge to the marksman (it has been clocked in flight at 75 miles per hour), and because it is a Chesapeake Bay tradition, the canvasback has sustained extremely heavy hunting pressure for the last 100 years. Even in closed seasons, the nondescript females are sometimes inadvertently shot, and there is illegal shooting and trapping. In addition to hunting pressure, conditions on the breeding grounds have been increasingly less favorable.

The principal breeding grounds of the canvasback are the Northern Plains States and the Prairie Provinces of Canada. Most of this area is

known as the "duck factory" and "pothole country." Specifically, this
would include southern Manitoba, southern Saskatchewan, southern
Alberta, northwestern Minnesota, and much of North Dakota. Here,
amid thousands of small shallow marshy lakes, ponds or potholes in the
"duck factory," is where the canvasback nests and raises its young (Fig.
70). Since the breeding area lies within the northern grain belt, one of
the limiting factors has been the reclamation of some of the pothole
areas for agricultural purposes. Remaining nesting ground areas,

Fig. 70. Hen canvasback protecting young from intrusion. Most canvasbacks nest in
the prairie pothole country of the Dakotas, Saskatchewan and Manitoba. Photograph by Jerome Stoudt, courtesy U.S. Fish and Wildlife Service.

whether on or off wildlife refuges and special areas maintained by
Ducks Unlimited, are subject to drought in some breeding seasons.
When ponds dry up during the nesting season, ducks may become dis-
couraged and abandon the area; or if they persist in nesting, they are
subject to heavy predation by skunks, foxes, and raccoons. Also, the
canvasback has a smaller breeding range than certain more abundant
waterfowl such as the mallard and black duck.

Just what effect the relatively recent disappearance of much of the vast beds of submerged aquatic vegetation in the Chesapeake Bay may have on wintering canvasback populations is a question mark. This situation is now being investigated by wildlife biologists. Where the food of the canvasback in the Chesapeake Bay area was formerly about 80 percent plant material, it is now about 80 percent animal matter.

Canvasbacks are presently feeding mostly on two species of small clams known as macoma and rangia. Since these small mollusks occur in great abundance in waters along the western shore of the Bay, the canvasback population has shifted more to that side in recent years. Major concentrations often occur in the central Potomac River area off Westmoreland and King George Counties, Virginia; in Maryland, near Baltimore Harbor; Gibson Island; Cove Point off Calvert County; the lower Choptank River; and Fishing Bay in Dorchester County. The western shore areas mentioned are some of the most polluted in the Bay. If the canvasback can make it in these waters, perhaps it can hold its own for a while.

SOMERSET MARSHES

Somerset and Worcester are the two southernmost counties on the Eastern Shore of Maryland. Worcester lies on the ocean side and Somerset on the Bay. Somerset is a bit more remote than the other Eastern Shore counties, which, as far as I am concerned, is in its favor.

Somerset County is known as the "rail capital of America" according to a recent article in *Maryland Birdlife* (32). On one December day in 1973, a party of bird watchers counted 129 Virginia rails, 63 king rails, 12 sora rails and 7 clapper rails in Somerset marshes.

Late in the springs of 1958, 1959 and 1960, when John Webb, my colleague in the U.S. Fish and Wildlife Service, and I were censusing nesting red-winged blackbird populations in tidal marshes of the Bay, one of the areas that we covered extensively was the marsh country of Somerset County. We boated the Big Annemessex, the Manokin, Pocomoke Sound, Ape Hole Creek, Marumsco and other waters to determine the density of breeding red-winged blackbird populations in various marsh types.

Down in this lower part of the Bay we found that the marshes are broader and saltier and the country is a little wilder; and there are offshore islands such as Bloodsworth's, South Marsh, Barren, and some smaller ones, that are uninhabited except during the ducking season. Because of the location and character of these natural landuse areas of Somerset, the variety of water birds probably exceeds that of any other county in the Maryland part of the Chesapeake Bay Country.

Of special interest to the ornithologist is the State's Deal Island Wildlife Management Area, which, despite its name, is not on Deal Island at all, but is located a few miles west of Princess Anne, near the village of Dames Quarter. This impounded marsh is managed for optimum waterfowl use, and therefore attracts not only ducks and geese but also rails, common gallinules, herons, egrets, and glossy ibis in considerable numbers. Diking and channeling have diversified the Deal Island Management Area by opening up what was formerly a rather sterile extensive needlerush marsh. Now the area has a greater variety of plant associations and ponds.

On the evening of July 11, 1974, Matthew Perry, a colleague of mine at the Patuxent Wildlife Research Center, and I walked across a section of this marsh toward a great blue heron nesting colony located perhaps a mile and a half from where our car was parked, and approximately due south of Dames Quarter. The section that we crossed was perhaps over a thousand acres in size and was composed predominantly of two species of plants, salt-marsh bulrush (Fig. 71) and salt grass, interrupted with little pools of different sizes and shapes. We flushed black ducks, blue-winged teal, and gadwalls from these ponds, some with broods

Fig. 71. Salt-marsh bulrush, common plant of brackish and salt marshes, forms extensive stands in a section of marsh near Dames Quarter, Somerset County, Maryland. It occurs in poorly drained areas often with considerable standing water at low tide.

(Fig. 72). A wide assortment of birds was encountered as we trudged toward the heronry, including great blue, little blue, Louisiana, green, black-crowned and yellow-crowned night herons, common, snowy, and cattle egrets, glossy ibis, least and American bitterns, common gallinule, Virginia and clapper rails, willets, greater yellowlegs, dunlins, black-bellied plover, killdeer, a pair of black skimmers, fish crows, marsh hawks, long-billed marsh wrens, seaside sparrows, boat-tailed grackles, and the ever present red-winged blackbirds. The great blue heron colony, located in a small group of tall dead trees, contained about 75 nests, some of which still had young.

There is a road beginning opposite the post office at Dames Quarter and leading out into the marsh for several miles along one of the dikes which makes a good and extended vantage ground for bird watching.

Fig. 72. Blue-winged teal hen leading brood across pond in Somerset County, Maryland, marsh, July 11, 1974. This section of marsh, located near Dames Quarter, is composed mostly of salt grass and salt-marsh bulrush. Photograph by Matthew C. Perry.

On September 10, 1974, I saw an estimated 2,000 blue-winged teal and three Hudsonian curlews or whimbrels from this dike; and out in the middle of the marsh in broad daylight, a red fox!

In contrast to the rich Deal Island Wildlife Management Area are the nearby extensive pure stands of natural marshlands, mostly composed of needlerush (Fig. 73), that have relatively low densities of bird species except where there is an interspersion of ponds that provide an edge

Fig. 73. Nest and eggs of marsh hawk in needlerush marsh near Dames Quarter, Somerset County, Maryland, June 15, 1961. Needlerush is one of the dominant plants in the extensive salt estuarine bay marsh of this area.

effect. Most of the birdlife of the needlerush area occurs along the tidal guts (Fig. 74) that wind through the marshes. These guts are usually lined with high-tide bush. Black ducks, blue-winged teal, long-billed marsh wrens, and seaside sparrows (Fig. 75) nest along the edges of the guts.

Along the upper reaches of the rivers and creeks of Somerset County, big cordgrass usually is predominant, indicating a change from a salt to a brackish environment. Some of these marshes provide a meeting

Fig. 74. Salt-marsh gut in Dames Quarter marsh, Somerset County, Maryland. Vegetation is mainly needlerush. Shrub at left foreground is hightide-bush. Summer habitat of clapper rail, black duck, blue-winged teal, seaside sparrow, and long-billed marsh wren.

ground for the king rail, an inhabitant of the fresher marshes, and the clapper rail, a salt-marsh bird. Big cordgrass deteriorates very little in winter; therefore, it is one of the best marsh cover types for wildlife at all seasons. I have seen over a million redwings roosting in this cover type in winter along Marumsco Creek in Somerset. Narrowleaf cattail (Fig. 76), found in fresh to slightly brackish areas here, is another tall marsh type that is an excellent all-season cover for wildlife.

Definitive ornithological investigations in Somerset County have been relatively recent, and a number of significant discoveries have been made there in the last 30 years. On May 19 and 20, 1948, Paul Springer

Fig. 75. Seaside sparrow perched on salt-marsh bulrush. This is the common sparrow of Chesapeake Bay salt marshes. Photograph by Luther Goldman.

and Robert E. Stewart discovered the first nests of the gadwall in Maryland (33). Most of these ducks nest in the Northern Plains States and Prairie Provinces of Canada. Harry Armistead, a Philadelphia ornithologist, discovered the first Maryland nests of the coot (August, 16, 1970) (34) and green-winged teal (June 5, 1971) (35) in Somerset marshes. Armistead has also made comprehensive surveys of heronries (nesting colonies of herons, egrets and glossy ibis) on offshore islands bordering Somerset and Dorchester Counties. The cluster of islands,

Fig. 76. Narrowleaf cattail has leaves about as wide as a pencil. In the Chesapeake Bay area it is a characteristic plant of extensive fresh and slightly brackish estuarine bay marshes. It is a good cover plant for marsh nesting birds.

beginning with Smith near the Virginia line and extending northward to Barren Island, have the most important heronries of mixed species in the Maryland section of the Chesapeake Bay. Armistead has written an interesting article about these island heronries in the March 1974 issue of *Maryland Birdlife* (36).

I have spent many hours in heronries gathering information on productivity, behavior, and banding young, and have found them to be exciting (but smelly!) places, particularly when they have young. Some of the young fall out of the nest and die and rot; and the young in nests often regurgitate their food when disturbed adding to the stench. When you walk under a nest of young herons or egrets, you take a chance of being hit on the head with a dead fish! But from a distance, heronries

Fig. 77. The common egret is one of the glamour birds of the Chesapeake Bay Country. Sizable nesting colonies of egrets, herons, and ibis are located on Barren, Bloodsworth, Smith, and some of the other offshore islands in the Chesapeake Bay opposite Dorchester and Somerset Counties. Photograph by Luther Goldman, U.S. Fish and Wildlife Service.

are spectacular, particularly when the predominantly white aggregation rises in a cloud over the colonial nesting site.

Herons, egrets and ibis, some of our most magnificent birds, are also among the most fragile (Fig. 77). They need more of man's protection than most other species. Their nesting colonies are especially vulnerable and can remain viable only when they are located in remote, uninhabited areas such as Somerset County offshore islands or in wildlife sanctuaries. Even in the best located heronries, predation on nest contents, particularly eggs, occurs. Raccoons may not be present on some islands out in the Bay, but fish crows pillage eggs at all heronries in tidewater areas.

I have visited fish crow feeding stations out in the Somerset and Dorchester marshes that were strewn with eggs of clapper and king rails, herons and egrets, and blue-winged teal and black ducks. The feeding site is usually an old pine stub, and occasionally the top of a duck blind. I have counted over 100 eggshells at some of these sites.

Fig. 78. Male boat-tailed grackles. The boat-tail is a southern maritime species that in the Chesapeake Bay Country reaches its northern limit in southern Dorchester County, near Fishing Bay. Photograph by Luther Goldman.

The boat-tailed grackle (Fig. 78), also a nest robber, is a bird unfamiliar to most Marylanders because of its limited distribution in the Chesapeake Bay Country and the Maryland coast. It is fairly common at Deal's Island and Rumbly. This species is essentially a southern bird that in the Bay area is found only as far north as Somerset and Dorchester Counties. It occurs up to about Fishing Bay near the village of

Elliott. Along the coast it occurs as far north as southern New Jersey. The male is black like a crow and about the same length, but is much slimmer. The brownish female is considerably smaller. The females form nesting colonies which the males visit for mating, much of which is promiscuous.

Boat-tailed grackles and fish crows are scavengers feeding around crab pots, on the offal around fish processing plants and at garbage dumps. Both species also forage in marshes in quest of crustaceans, amphibians, and other aquatic animal life.

Most of this narrative has been about the native or summer birdlife of Somerset marshes. The abundance and variety of birds that occur there in summer are considerably augmented with the onset of southward migration which is well under way in August. The migration season finds thousands of shorebirds, ducks, other forms of water birds and land birds concentrating in and near Somerset marshes. They stop over to feed and rest before continuing their southward journey down the Chesapeake, which because of its north-south direction is a major migratory flyway.

OF DUCKS, GEESE, AND SWAN

The Chesapeake Bay winters about 5 percent of the continental waterfowl population and about 25 percent of those that follow the Atlantic Flyway. The total number of waterfowl wintering in the Bay region has probably changed very little in the last 20 years from the estimated one million waterfowl reported in the mid-1950s.

Fig. 79. "Wings set for landing." Canada geese occur in greater numbers in the Chesapeake Bay area than in any other locality in their winter range. Photograph by P.J. Van Huizen.

Much of what is known about the numbers, distribution, and ecology of waterfowl in the Chesapeake Bay is contained in the report by Robert E. Stewart, entitled "Waterfowl Populations in the Upper Chesapeake Region" (37). The information in that report is based on data gathered in the 1950s. At the time of Stewart's survey, diving ducks (canvasback, redhead, scaup, ruddy duck, common goldeneye, and bufflehead) were most numerous, making up 42 percent of the

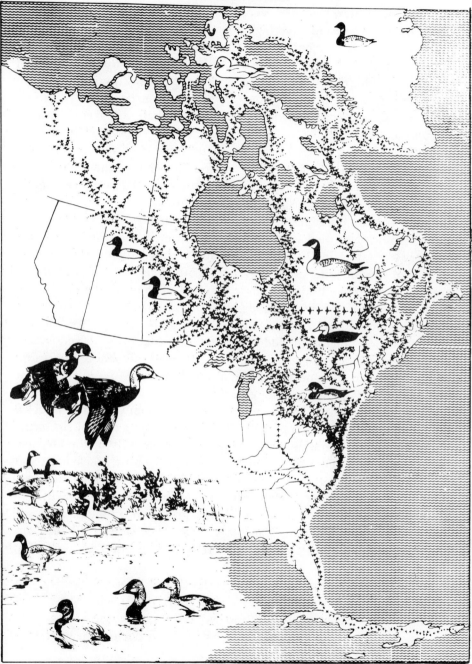

Fig. 80. Atlantic Flyway, showing migration routes of waterfowl from the breeding grounds to the Chesapeake Bay. Illustration by Bob Hines, U.S. Fish and Wildlife Service.

population. Others, in order, were dabbling ducks (black, mallard, widgeon, blue-winged and green-winged teal, shoveler, and gadwall), 29 percent; geese, 18 percent; swan, 4 percent; coots (members of the rail family, but classed as waterfowl in the hunting regulations), 3 percent; sea ducks (old-squaws and scoters) and mergansers, 2 percent; and unidentified ducks, 2 percent. The canvasback, Canada goose (Fig. 79), black duck, and scaup made up more than half the average winter population. Populations of several species have fluctuated in the ensuing years, and today (1974) the percentage of Canada geese and mallards in the Bay area would be greater, and that of the divers somewhat lower. It is of interest to note that the Canada goose, black duck, whistling swan, and canvasback usually occur in greater numbers during the winter in the Chesapeake Bay region than in any other locality.

The majority of ducks and geese that winter in the Chesapeake Bay Country are raised in Canada. Figure 80 illustrates the routes of migration from the breeding grounds. At least 50 percent of our game ducks are produced in the prairie pothole country of the Canadian provinces of Saskatchewan, Manitoba, and Alberta, and the states of North Dakota and Minnesota. Pincipal species of waterfowl produced in the prairie pothole region include the mallard, blue-winged and green-winged teal, pintail, shoveler, widgeon, redhead, canvasback, and scaup. The parkland region north of the pothole country is an important nesting habitat of scaup and goldeneye; and the arctic tundra and northern bush country are breeding grounds of some of the sea ducks, the scoters, old-squaws, and the mergansers. In years of drought in the pothole country, some ducks that usually nest there fly beyond to nest in the great river deltas of the far north, the Athabasca, Mackenzie, and Great Slave Lake region. Our most abundant duck, the mallard, nests throughout all three of the waterfowl breeding areas mentioned. The black duck, number one in our flyway, is produced from eastern Canada to North Carolina; and Canada geese of the Atlantic Flyway are raised mostly in eastern Canada, many from the Hudson Bay-James Bay region.

Following the nesting season and summer molt, some ducks begin to move toward the Chesapeake Bay country by late August. These early arrivals are the blue-winged teal and wood ducks that seek the fresher marshes of our estuaries. They join some wood ducks that were produced locally in our river bottom forests.

By September a few mallards and pintails are beginning to appear in these same marshes. Waterfowl increase markedly in late October and

November, reaching a peak in December, as both transient and wintering populations concentrate in the upper Chesapeake Bay area.

Chesapeake Bay, largest estuary in the country, has the broad areas
of fresh, brackish, and salt tidal waters, the thousands of acres of
marshlands, and the food source to support several million ducks and
geese during the winter half of the year. Submerged aquatic flora ("sea-
weed"), an important food of a number of waterfowl, is in short supply
now, but some ducks such as the canvasback that depended heavily on

Fig. 81. Pintails on pond bordering the Potomac River, just south of Washington,
D.C. Photograph by Frank Dufresne, courtesy of the U.S. Fish and Wildlife Service.

this food source in the past have appeared to have done fairly well by
shifting to mollusks or other aquatic animal life. The impact of the
shortage of submerged aquatics is not well known. It would certainly
have an effect on local distribution. On the other hand, crop residues in
grain fields are much greater today with the advent of the mechanical
harvester, and some waterfowl are taking advantage of this bonanza. As
much as 5 percent of the corn is left in many harvested fields, and this
is the primary reason that we now have more mallards and Canada geese
wintering on the Eastern Shore of Maryland.

In years past, the Susquehanna Flats, a fresh estuarine bay type, was an important area for swan and also canvasback, until the wild celery disappeared when hurricane "Agnes" came through and scoured the shallow water area, causing a turbidity or muddying of the waters. In the last few years it has seemed strange to see swan out in crop fields feeding on the young shoots of winter wheat, a shift probably resulting from a general shortage of underwater aquatic plants in much of the Bay area.

Fig. 82. A cold January day on the Potomac River, looking from Charles County, Maryland, toward King George County, Virginia. This brackish estuarine section of the central Potomac is an important wintering area for canvasback, scaup, and ruddy ducks.

In the upper Chesapeake Bay, the brackish estuarine bay type is the most important habitat for waterfowl. According to Stewart (ibid), in the 1950s, between one-half and three-fifths of the late fall-winter population was found in this habitat. Large numbers of Canada geese, mallards, pintails (Fig. 81) and blacks concentrate in brackish estuarine bays that are adjacent to agricultural fields along the eastern shore of

Chesapeake Bay in the Chester River, Eastern Bay, and Choptank River sections. The waterfowl of these areas feed on corn and other waste grains left from the fall harvest operation, as well as in the offshore shoalwaters. In 1974 this was still the best waterfowl area in the Bay. Over one-half of the Bay's swan population occurs in this area where they traditionally have fed mostly on submerged aquatic plants and thin-shelled mollusks, the long clam "soft-shelled" and Baltic macoma.

Fig. 83. Matt Perry and Don White, of the U.S. Fish and Wildlife Service, bottom sampling for mollusks in the Tangier Sound area. Mollusks are an important food of diving ducks in many areas of the Bay.

Another brackish estuarine area of considerable waterfowl importance is the central portion of the Potomac River (Fig. 82) from about the mouth of the Port Tobacco River to the mouth of the Wicomico

River. Although somewhat polluted, it is still one of the best concentration areas in the Chesapeake Bay system for canvasbacks, scaup, and
ruddy ducks. Small clams are the principal food of these divers in this
area.

Salt estuarine bay habitat, mostly adjacent to Dorchester and Somerset Counties in the upper Bay, but also including the lower part of the
western shore of the Maryland section, includes the best areas for some
of the other divers: the common goldeneye, bufflehead, and redhead,
and for the sea ducks, the old-squaw and the scoters, and also a few
brant. Goldeneyes, buffleheads, and old-squaws feed mostly on mol-

Fig. 84. Winter at Allen's Fresh, near the head of Wicomico River, in Charles
County, Maryland. On the February day in 1958 that this photograph was made,
the only signs of life in this frozen marsh were a few song and swamp sparrows,
one red-winged blackbird and the tracks of a king rail.

lusks, crustaceans, and fish. Old-squaws are deep divers that often get
caught in gill nets. Scoters, the common, white-winged, and surf species
(also known as sea coots) are our largest ducks. Mollusks form their
principal diet (Fig. 83).

In severe winters (Fig. 84), many waterfowl from the upper Bay area
move down where the saltier waters remain open. The open water of
the Salt Estuarine Bays include, among others, Pocomoke Sound (Fig.
85), Big Annemessex, Manokin, and Honga Rivers, Tar Bay, Tangier
Sound, Mobjack Bay, and the lower James River.

Fig. 85. Pocomoke Sound, lying between Somerset County, Maryland, and Accomac County, Virginia, is a Salt Estuarine Bay type used by such diving ducks as old-squaw, bufflehead, and common goldeneye.

Fig. 86. Brackish pond on Kent Island, Queen Annes County, Maryland, covered with widgeon grass, one of the most important foods of dabbling ducks in the Chesapeake Bay Country.

Extensive brackish marshes, especially in Dorchester and Somerset Counties, are an important fall and winter habitat for such dabblers or puddle ducks as the black, widgeon, green-winged teal, gadwall, shoveler, and also the hooded merganser. One of the best areas is the Blackwater-Nanticoke area, which includes Blackwater National Wildlife Refuge and the vast Elliott Island marsh. These areas and the Deal Island marsh, south of Dames Quarter in Somerset County, are some of our finest black duck and blue-winged teal breeding marshes.

Principal foods of waterfowl in the brackish estuarine marshes usually are widgeon grass (Fig. 86) and the salt-marsh snail. Other kinds of aquatic plants and animals are utilized to some extent. In the less brackish sections of the vast bay marshes, Canada geese vie with the muskrat in their use of the rootstocks of Olney three-square.

Fresh tidal river marshes, such as those of the Patuxent near Upper Marlboro, the Elk River at the head of the Bay, and the Chickahominy, Mattaponi, and Pamunkey Rivers in the Virginia section, are excellent waterfowl areas, especially early in the season when the smartweeds and wildrice seed production is at its height in early September.

A rating of important waterfowl foods in the Atlantic Coastal region today would be somewhat different from one made in the 1930s by Martin and Uhler in their book, "Food of Game Ducks in the United States and Canada" (38). Submerged aquatic plants were more important 40 years ago, where today marine animals and corn probably rate highest. Martin and Uhler's list and a present-day tentative list of the author, based on field and laboratory studies, make for an interesting comparison:

1930s	1970s
pondweeds (submerged aquatic plants)	bivalves
snails	snails
wild celery (submerged aquatic plant)	corn
widgeon grass " " "	crustaceans
bivalves (clams)	widgeon grass
crustaceans (shrimp, crabs, and relatives)	bulrushes
smartweeds (emergent aquatic plants)	smartweeds
bulrushes " " "	Olney three-square
eelgrass (submerged aquatic plant)	pondweeds
corn	wheat (mainly sprouts)

As Stewart notes in his work, foods of waterfowl vary from one species to another and from one habitat to another. Variations in foods utilized by any given species appear to be due to differences in availability of foods and so are influenced by habitat and seasonal changes. For the majority of waterfowl in the 1950s, Stewart thought that widgeon grass probably was the most important single waterfowl food in the upper Chesapeake Bay region.

In addition to a deterioration of the plant food source in the Bay region, hunting pressure, disturbance on the wintering grounds due to an increasing human population, reclamation of breeding marshes and ponds for agricultural purposes, and droughts in the prairie provinces of Canada are all factors that are having a depressing effect on the national waterfowl population.

In 1941 there were an estimated 71 million waterfowl in North America. This figure represents a remarkable comeback from the estimated 30 million in 1934, a population low resulting from droughts on the Canadian prairie breeding grounds. Today's pressures on the environment lessen the possibility of any increase in the present population of an estimated 25 million wintering waterfowl. The establishment of additional wildlife refuges and private sanctuaries in recent years, a program of creating artificial nest structures for wood ducks, blacks, and mallards, and the general stability of arctic and subarctic breeding grounds where most of our geese and some of our ducks are produced, should assure us of a huntable population for some years to come.

THE LOWER JAMES

The Lower James River Country may well be considered the birthplace of North American ornithology. It was at Jamestown that Mark Catesby, the first serious student of birds in this country, arrived in 1712 to begin his collections, drawings, and descriptions of the fauna and flora of our South Atlantic Coastal region. While the title of his distinguished published work is "The Natural History of Carolina, Florida, and the Bahama Islands" (39), Catesby's first impressions were of Virginia birds and plants. Some of the plates in Catesby's book were copies of drawings made during his residence in Virginia. Among the North American birds that he gets credit for discovering while living in Virginia, are the Baltimore oriole (he called it the Baltimore-Bird), the redstart (his Red-Start), mockingbird (The Mock-Bird), and the catbird (Cat-Bird) (40). The extinct Carolina parakeet should probably be added to this list. This brilliantly-colored red, yellow, and green bird was our only native parrot. It was a southern species that reached its northeastern limit in the vicinity of the Potomac River. Apparently it was fairly common about Jamestown at certain seasons. The last parakeets known to exist were seen in southern Florida, in 1920 (41).

During his seven years in the Virginia colony, Catesby became a good friend of Colonel William Byrd II, and spent a number of days examining plants at Westover, the distinguished statesman's plantation on the James. Catesby lived for a time with his brother-in-law, Dr. William Cocke, also an eminent statesman, who was one of Her Majesty's councilors in the Colony.

As Witmer Stone, late Curator of Birds at the Academy of Natural Science in Philadelphia, stated in a paper in the *Auk* (42), Mark Catesby's work in the South Atlantic area formed the "basis of the ornithology not only in the Southern States, but the whole of North America. . . ."

But the first reports on birds in the Colony, while brief, were made by the pioneer settlers at Jamestown, a hundred years or so before Catesby's arrival. George Percy (1607), Captain John Smith (1612), and William Stachey (1610-1612) made notes in their journals about the "divers sortes of hawkes, quailes, parakitoes, a kind of wood-pidgeon [the now extinct passenger pigeon], divers diving fowles and some other straunge kyndes, to us unknowne by name" (40).

124

Indeed Jamestown Island may have been chosen for a settlement not only for protection against the Indians, but additionally because of the vast marshes about the area that would have attracted a variety and abundance of waterfowl, an important source of food, particularly in the winter half of the year.

Fig. 87. The Chickahominy River, in Virginia tidewater country, is a tributary of the James. Extensive wildrice marshes, giant cutgrass near its northern limit, and bald cypress along its shoreline, are among the characteristic features of the Chickahominy. Note cones on cypress trees.

The James River Country is one of the fine waterfowl areas in Tidewater Virginia. Marsh ducks, or dabblers, are the most important from the hunters' standpoint. Dabbling ducks, the mallard, black, pintail, shoveler, and blue-winged and green-winged teal are usually found in or near marshes with a good seed production of smartweed, tearthumb, millet, wild rice, and rice cutgrass. Most of the marshes along the James, and its tributary rivers and creeks as far downstream as Jamestown, are fresh or only slightly brackish.

The Chickahominy, that enters the James about five miles above Jamestown, has the finest marshes in the James River system. They are largely fresh because the flow of the James past its mouth is still rather

Fig. 88. Typical growth of bald cypress along the Chickahominy River.

rapid. The Chickahominy has some of the most extensive wildrice marshes in the Chesapeake Bay area. When I visited the Gordon's Creek marsh on September 19, 1974, wild rice was at the height of seed production and red-winged blackbirds were taking their share and scattering enough for the sora rails and blue-winged teal that stop over for a few weeks in late summer and early fall on their southward migration.

Most of the fresh tidal river marshes in the Chesapeake Bay system are similar in character, with essentially the same plant species; but the Chickahominy marshes are distinguished by the occurrence of two additional marsh plants of warm temperate climates; one is giant cut-grass, a dominant plant of South Atlantic tidal marshes, and the other is Asiatic dayflower, an exotic.

Another interesting feature of the Chickahominy is its cypress-studded shoreline (Figs. 87 & 88). I have not noticed such a predominance of cypress along the shorelines of other tidal rivers in Virginia, but the shoreline of the Pocomoke River on Maryland's Eastern Shore is similarly lined with bald cypress trees.

From a few miles south of Richmond to the mouth of the James there are several areas that have notable waterfowl populations. Presque Isle National Wildlife Refuge, near Hopewell, and Hog Island State Wildlife Refuge, almost opposite Jamestown on the south shore of the River (Fig. 89), attract 5,000-10,000 Canada geese each winter, along with numerous dabblers. Judging from the number of duck blinds around Jamestown Island and the mouth of Powhatan Creek, which flows by the Island, good hunting continues in the tradition of the early settlers.

The mouth of the James, at Hampton Roads, presents a different waterfowl picture, one that finds the sea ducks, the three species of scoters (white-winged, surf, and common) and the old-squaw (or south-southerly), as well as other divers, the common goldeneye and buffle-head. The lower Nansemond River (Fig. 90), across from Hampton Roads, is a good concentration area for canvasbacks, ruddies, ring-necked ducks (Fig. 91), and red-breasted mergansers.

Marshes along the creeks and rivers, from about Jamestown downstream, are often dominated by big cordgrass and tidemarsh hemp, brackish water indicators. When waters approach sea salinity, these two plants disappear. Big cordgrass reaches an average height of about 7 or 8 feet, and unlike many of the more succulent marsh plants that deteriorate in late fall, it maintains its life-form through the winter. It was an important plant for the early settlers as it could be used for thatching roofs; today it is used to camouflage duck blinds. While of no food value to wildlife, big cordgrass is an excellent cover type as it forms extensive pure stands of optimum density. It is the dominant plant along the upper reaches of the Pagan River, at Smithfield, and the Nansemond, at Suffolk. Big cordgrass marshes are the favorite roosting places of red-winged blackbirds in the James River area.

The several species of blackbirds are the most abundant birds in the Lower James River Country. From my impressions of the writings of the first Jamestown colonists, the "black byrd with redd shoulders" was the first bird observed by the pioneers on arriving at the Island.

Fig. 89. A view of the James from Hog Island, looking toward Jamestown. Hog Island is a state waterfowl management area.

Fig. 90. Early morning on the Nansemond. The Nansemond River flows through Suffolk, Virginia, entering the James just above Norfolk. This photograph was made in September 1974, near Chuckatuck.

In the early days of Jamestown, this species was no doubt the most abundant bird in the marshes about the colony, but redwing numbers (Fig. 92) have increased manyfold since then because of the opening up of the country for agricultural crop production. Red-winged blackbirds

Fig. 91. The ring-necked duck is mainly a transient in the Chesapeake Bay Country. Most of them winter in the South. Photograph by Matthew C. Perry.

are essentially granivorous birds and, even before Jamestown, were raiding the fields of maize planted by the Indians.

Blackbirds are diurnal migrants that follow waterways and the coast-line; and the general north-south trend of Chesapeake Bay and the northwest-southeast direction of Virginia's major tidal rivers have the effect of funneling myriads of blackbirds into the Lower James River basin near the mouth of the Bay. Thus, in the fall there is a buildup, or ganging-up, of blackbirds in an area where there is an abundant food source, a milder climate, and adequate roosting cover in the big cord-grass marshes and in the Dismal Swamp.

During the late 1950s and early 1960s, several of us working for the U.S. Fish and Wildlife Service covered the Lower James River basin in

Fig. 92. Red-winged blackbirds assembled in tree prior to descending on harvested grainfields to feed on crop residue. Several million blackbirds winter along the Lower James where they roost in tidal marshes or fly 25 to 30 miles from the feeding grounds to Dismal Swamp to spend the night.

our southern winter blackbird roost surveys. The largest roost in the area was in the Dismal Swamp, which is located a few miles south of Norfolk. There were at least 25 million birds in the roost, about 50 percent of which were redwings. At the time, this was the largest black-bird roost in the country. Other winter roosts in the area, all located along the Lower James and its tributaries, were located in marshes and had the following estimated numbers: Bermuda Hundred, 100,000; Jamestown Island, 500,000; Pagan River, 20,000; and Nansemond River, 100,000. The majority of blackbirds in the river marsh roosts also were redwings.

Peanut culture in the Lower James River basin is one of the reasons for the concentration of millions of blackbirds in this area in fall and winter. Until recently, when dug from the ground in early fall, peanuts were stacked in five-foot-high shocks (Fig. 93) to dry out for a month or six weeks prior to threshing and storing. The fall arrival of northern migrant blackbirds coincided precisely with peanut-stacking time. Although it might seem as though the entire peanut crop was exposed to the hordes of blackbirds in the area for a considerable period of

Fig. 93. Shocked peanuts drying in a field in Surry County, Virginia, near the James River, October 1958. When harvested by this method, peanuts were vulnerable to depredations by blackbirds, blue jays and flickers. Today, most peanuts are artificially dried and not left in fields for a month or so, as formerly.

time, only peanuts on the outside of the shocks were vulnerable to foraging blackbirds. During the same period, the birds were also gleaning the peanuts left scattered on the ground from the digging operation. Blackbirds along the Lower James vary their diet, feeding on a host of food items, including corn, sorghum, weed seeds (such as ragweed and foxtail grass), and insects.

Today most of the peanut crop is dried artificially indoors, so the blackbird problem of the peanut grower is virtually nonexistent. A few fields of seed peanuts are still left in shocks in the field to dry. I have been told that a farmer is paid a penny more per pound for peanuts that have been dried by the "sunshine-and-fresh-air" process. Perhaps this adds a degree of quality.

On occasion, I have been a mile or two out in the Dismal Swamp where I have seen an old peanut shell or two lying on the ground. This probably happens when blackbirds, flying toward the roost in the evening, make one last stop at a field next to the Swamp and fly off with a peanut to be consumed at a resting place en route.

Blue jays, flickers, fish crows, common crows, and four species of gulls join blackbirds in feeding on peanuts left scattered on the ground from the fall harvest operation. I have seen over 100 flickers (a species of woodpecker), feeding on the ground in peanut fields; sometimes they are taking insects, as are the other birds mentioned here.

I have often wondered at the distance some blackbirds will fly from their roost before descending to feed. They obviously like to get out and get going, for they usually pass up a good food source only a short distance from the roost. I have followed a line of blackbirds for 30 miles from the Nansemond River roost to feeding grounds near Waverly, and they were passing over comparable foraging areas all along the way.

In my opinion, the millions of blackbirds that concentrate their foraging activity in the Lower James River Country during the winter half of the year offer the most impressive ornithological sight in the area. Perhaps the thousands of gulls that visit the harvested peanut fields are, at times or in some places, more conspicuous than the blackbirds. Although fish and other forms of seafood may comprise the major portion of their diet, gulls are omnivorous feeders. When they visit crop fields bordering the river, they are foraging for peanut residue, worms, grubs, and grasshoppers, depending upon the season. The sight of gulls following the plow as the sod is broken is a familiar one in tidewater country (Fig. 94).

There are four species that occur regularly along the Lower James: the herring, ring-billed, great black-backed, and laughing gulls. The laughing gull is the smallest of the four and can be distinguished from the others by its black head. It is the only native gull, nesting locally on the coastal marsh islands along the Eastern Shore of Virginia. The great black-backed is the least abundant and a relatively recent invader of this area whereas 50 years ago it was an extremely rare bird. The herring and ring-billed are the most common.

Blackbirds by the millions and gulls by the thousands are impressive enough to attract the attention of almost anyone. Twenty years ago I was impressed by the number of bald eagles that I saw along the Lower

James. This was one of their strongholds in the Chesapeake Bay Country. Today they are conspicuous by their absence.

Jackson Abbott (4) and collaborators, who make an annual bald eagle survey in the Chesapeake Bay area, have documented the decline of our national bird along the Lower James: "Speaking of rivers, the situation along the Chickahominy-James River system in Virginia is tragic. As recently as 1964 there were 13 pairs nesting along this river

Fig. 94. Laughing gulls following a disc harrow in search of insects and insect larvae. Photograph by Bob Jones, courtesy of U.S. Fish and Wildlife Service.

system. The number dropped to 11 pairs in 1965, 7 pairs in 1966, 5 pairs in 1967 through 1969, 4 pairs in 1970, 2 pairs in 1971, and just 1 pair in 1972 and 1973. Throughout these years only 1 pair produced young (1 eaglet in 1964, 1965, and 1969). In 1963, an adult eagle was picked up under a nest tree on Jamestown Island; the bird was deathly sick, trembling all over, and later died. Its body was autopsied at the Patuxent Wildlife Research Center in Maryland and was found to have DDT residues in its organs ranging from 6.9 parts per million (ppm) in the brain to a high of 34.3 ppm in the heart."

The demise of the bald eagle in the Chesapeake Bay Country is due to a pollution of the environment and various population pressures.

The waters about Norfolk, the meeting place of the James, the Bay and the ocean, have the effect of concentrating a fabulous array of seabirds and their allies in the Virginia Capes area. P.A. Buckley and F.G. Buckley have authored two fairly recent papers on this subject (43, 44) in the *Raven,* journal of the Virginia Society of Ornithology. The Buckleys describe the Norfolk region as "one of the most diverse in Virginia in terms of birds found as breeders, migrants, winter residents, or vagrants." Their records of interesting birds from the Virginia Capes area include the king and common eiders and the harlequin duck, three species of ducks that breed mostly in the arctic and are very rare south of Long Island in winter; six species of pelagic gulls, the glaucous, black-headed, little, lesser black-backed, kittiwake, and Sabine's; and a bird from the tropical seas, the frigate bird, or man-o'-war bird.

The Lower James River Country is as rich in birdlife as it is in history. Mark Catesby came to a bountiful area to begin his career as America's pioneer scientific ornithologist.

SOME OTHER OBSERVATIONS

Although I have not made a thorough assessment of state bird records, I believe that more unusual birds are seen in the Chesapeake Bay Country than elsewhere in Maryland and Virginia. The fact that birds tend to follow extensive north-south trending bodies of water in their migrations and wanderings is doubtless one explanation for the numerous records in the Bay area. Another reason may be that there are more bird watchers (both native and migrant!) making observations in that

Fig. 95. Saw-whet owl. Jan Reese and collaborators caught 29 of these little owls in mist nets at Kent Point, one early October morning. This was, indeed, an unusual ornithological event. Illustration by John W. Taylor.

135

area than anywhere else in Maryland and Virginia. Consider, too, the visibility of most water birds, and the long uninterrupted sweeps of marsh and shore which one often can view from one spot, and it would be remarkable, indeed, if another area could claim as many sightings of wanderers.

In our earlier years of birding some of the birds that we thought were only occasional visitors have since been found to occur regularly at certain seasons. The saw-whet owl is an example. Some other species are of cyclic occurrence, e.g., the snowy owl.

In the late 1950s, one of the techniques that I used for capturing red-winged blackbirds for banding purposes was to place Japanese mist nets near a huge blackbird roost located in the Patuxent River marsh. The nets were set at dusk after the birds had settled in the roost for the night. They were visited the following morning at about sunrise as the blackbirds were leaving the roost. The technique worked quite well and often other species, such as swamp and song sparrows, and an occasional sora or bobolink, were netted along with the redwings. One October morning I was surprised when I found a saw-whet owl (Fig. 95) in one of the nets. This little owl breeds in the north country and in our higher Appalachians, and visits eastern sections of Maryland in the fall and winter. At that time, a record of a saw-whet owl in eastern Maryland was an event worthy of note. However, ten years later, with an increase in mist netting activity by a number of birdbanders in marshes and along the better established migration routes of the Bay shore, these little owls were found to be fairly common in fall and winter.

In an article entitled "An Unprecedented Concentration of Saw-whet Owls," in the June 1966 issue of *Maryland Birdlife* (45), Jan Reese reported the capture of 29 of these owls in mist nets one early October morning at a banding station located at Kent Point, on the southern tip of Kent Island. This was the largest number of saw-whet owls captured at one time in Maryland.

According to Jan, there was a good flight of several other species the previous day, when the weather was clear and the temperature reached a balmy 76 degrees. Then, Jan wrote:

"That evening the wind changed from NNE at 10 m.p.h. to ENE at 18 m.p.h. and the temperature dipped to a chilly 45 degrees during the night. These very favorable conditions provoked a terrific flight of fall migrants during the night and we were capturing goodly numbers of birds as early as two hours prior to sunrise on the 17th.

" . . . We were blessed with the presence of these personable little birds [saw-whets] all day as they preferred not to fly far when released. Instead they viewed us from nearby tree branches and low bushes. Several were recaptured by hand during the day for study and photography by visitors.

" . . . I am sure that morning will be long remembered by all participants and the Bridges will probably never forgive us for having such a good day at the O.R. station."

On that fabulous day, Jan Reese and some friends were subbing for David and Margaret Bridge at their "Operation Recovery" birdbanding station at Kent Point.

As mentioned elsewhere, another method that I use for capturing blackbirds for banding and experimental studies is the decoy enclosure trap (Fig. 96). Most of my traps are 20 x 40 feet and six feet in height.

Fig. 96. Blackbird decoy trap at the Patuxent Wildlife Research Center used for capturing birds for banding purposes. Live decoys are left in trap to attract other blackbirds which enter trap through opening in top. Bait is placed beneath top opening.

A dozen or two live blackbirds are kept in the trap as decoys. The trap is baited with cracked corn placed on the ground beneath an opening in the top. This type of trap is pretty selective for blackbirds, but other species occasionally enter.

On October 13, 1967, a yellow-headed blackbird, a western species, joined the red-winged blackbird decoy flock in one of my decoy enclosure traps. The yellow-head is a bird of the pothole marshes of the

Great Plains and some far western valley marshes. At the time, my bird, an immature male (Fig. 97), was only the third recorded occurrence of this species in Maryland in the present century. There are three records from the 1890s, all from the wildrice marshes (no longer existing) south of Baltimore Harbor near the present Hanover Street Bridge.

Fig. 97. Immature male yellow-headed blackbird caught in blackbird decoy trap at the Patuxent Wildlife Research Center, October 13, 1967. This western species has been observed in Maryland only about a half dozen times.

My yellow-head was shown to about 50 persons, some of whom came to see it after an announcement of its capture was made on a local radio station. The bird was banded and released, never to be heard from again. Since only about one percent of all banded blackbirds are recovered, this was not unexpected.

The lark bunting, another bird of the western Great Plains was observed by my colleagues John Webb, Robert Mitchell, and me while censusing red-winged blackbirds in the marshes of Slaughter Creek in Dorchester County. This bird, a male, was observed on July 10, 1958, at a time when it should have been on nesting grounds in the rolling country of western Kansas or Nebraska. I knew the sighting to be unusual, so it was collected and placed in the U.S. National Museum collections. It proved to be the first record for the State.

For some unexplained reasons, certain songbirds that are supposed to be in the tropics in the middle of winter occasionally show up at our bird feeders. John W. (Bud) Taylor, the Chesapeake Bay waterfowl artist who lives by Selby Bay, south of Annapolis, phoned me one frigid January day asking me to come see a yellow warbler at his bird feeder. Knowing that this was probably the first winter record of the yellow warbler in Maryland, I hurried over and spent the morning at Bud's studio window witnessing this rare sight. The little shivering yellow bird was feeding on pieces of sunflower seed dropped by sparrows when they cracked open the seed coats and plucked at the kernels. It continued to visit Bud's feeder daily for about a week.

But, of all the unusual birds that show up in the Chesapeake Bay Country, none arouse as much excitement among bird watchers as the snowy owl (Fig. 98). Although they have been recorded in the literature as occurring in Maryland during a number of winters in the last hundred years, more birders will dash out and travel many miles to see this big spectacular bird from the arctic than will make an effort to see some smaller and less engaging species observed in Maryland for the first time. When Bud Taylor and I went to South River, a short distance from Annapolis, in January 1974, to see a snowy owl perched on a rooftop, there were already ten carloads of birders there ahead of us. The owl remained in the area for about four days, where it perched mainly on rooftops, chimneys and channel markers.

Snowy owls usually move down to the States when lemmings and hares, their staple food in the far north country, are in short supply. A major "invasion" occurred in the winter of 1926-27, when 2,363 were recorded in an area extending into the Great Lakes region, the New England and Middle Atlantic States, and as far south as North Carolina

Fig. 98. The snowy owl, a rare winter bird from the arctic, attracts a great deal of attention from bird watchers when it visits the Chesapeake Bay area. This photograph was made by Hal Wierenga in January 1974, at South River, near Annapolis.

(46). Twelve were reported from Maryland at that time. During the incursion of 1949-50, at least 25 were recorded in Maryland (9). During the winter of 1936, I knew of six that were caught in pole traps on Spesutie Island, in the upper Chesapeake area. The Island at the time was a private hunting club and such birds of prey were kept in check because of ring-necked pheasants introduced for hunting.

The owls often arrive in starving condition and, according to Frank L. Kenny of the Turnbull National Wildlife Refuge, one snowy owl near Baranga, Michigan, swooped down and made off with a squirrel's tail flying from an auto radio aerial; another tried to take the fur hat off of a Canadian game warden (47).

It is usually assumed that most invading snowy owls occur near tidewater because of the abundance of waterfowl, a convenient source of food. However, many owls shot during the 1926-27 invasion were found to be feeding on rats. Perhaps the north-south direction of the great waterways of the northeast, Chesapeake Bay, Delaware Bay, Hudson River, Connecticut River, Lake Champlain and other waters to the north, act as a natural flyway in funneling the flight southward from the North Country.

I have mentioned only a few examples of the many unusual birds that have been reported in the Chesapeake Bay Country. Most of the sightings are made during the annual Christmas Counts in Maryland, in which there may be 500-600 bird counters; in summer, when there is a lot of postnesting season-wandering (particularly of southern birds northward), and during hurricanes when birds of the tropical seas—frigate birds, white-tailed tropic birds, sooty terns and others—are blown up the coast and often inland for some miles.

Birdwatching is becoming so sophisticated in the Chesapeake Bay Country these days that if a rare or unusual bird comes near our shores it is not long before someone has "the book on it." A Hudsonion godwit, large shorebird with an upturned bill, that seldom graces Dorchester County marshes, arrived at Blackwater National Wildlife Refuge on October 26, about one month late for that latitude. Kathy Klimkiewicz, one of our more astute bird watchers, saw the bird and a few days later came over to the Patuxent Wildlife Research Center where I work to report her rare sighting.

When some of the birders at the Center indicated an interest in seeing it, Kathy crushed their euphoria by stating that the bird left Blackwater at exactly 1:22 p.m. on the 28th. As the interest in birding increases in the Chesapeake Bay area the heretofore private wanderings of birds are no longer very secret.

APPENDIX

Common and Scientific Names of Birds

bittern, American *(Botaurus lentigenosus)*
  least *(Ixobrychus exilis)*
blackbird, red-winged *(Agelaius phoeniceus)*
  rusty *(Euphagus carolinus)*
  yellow-headed *(Xanthocephalus xanthocephalus)*
bluebird, eastern *(Sialia sialis)*
bobolink, *(Dolichonyx oryzivorus)*
brant, Atlantic *(Branta bernicla)*
bufflehead *(Bucephala albeola)*
bunting, lark *(Calamospiza melanocorys)*

canvasback *(Aythya valisineria)*
cardinal, *(Richmondena cardinalis)*
catbird *(Dumetella carolinensis)*
chickadee, Carolina *(Parus carolinensis)*
chuck-will's-widow *(Caprimulgus carolinensis)*
coot, American *(Fulica americana)*
crow, common *(Corvus brachyrhynchos)*
  fish *(Corvus ossifragus)*
curlew, Hudsonian *(Numenius phaeopus)*

dowitcher *(Limnodromus griseus)*
duck, black *(Anas rubripes)*
  harlequan *(Histrionicus histrionicus)*
  ring-necked *(Aythya collaris)*
duck, ruddy *(Oxyura jamaicensis)*
  wood *(Aix sponsa)*
dunlin *(Erolia alpina)*

eagle, bald *(Haliaeetus leucocephalus)*
egret, cattle *(Bubulcus ibis)*
  common *(Casmerodius albus)*
  snowy *(Leucophoyx thula)*
eider, common *(Somateria mollissima)*
  king *(Somateria spectabilis)*

flicker, yellow-shafted *(Colaptes auratus)*
frigate bird *(Fregata magnificens)*

gadwall *(Anas strepera)*
gallinule, common *(Gallinula chloropus)*
  purple *(Porphyrula martinica)*
godwit, Hudsonian *(Limosa haemastica)*
goldeneye, common *(Bucephala clangula)*

goose, Canada *(Branta canadensis)*
  greater snow *(Chen hyperborea atlantica)*
  lesser snow *(Chen hyperborea)*
grackle, common *(Quiscalus quiscula)*
  boat-tailed *(Cassidix mexicanus)*
grebe, horned *(Podiceps auritus)*
gull, black-headed *(Larus ridibundus)*
  glaucous *(Larus hyperboreus)*
  great black-backed *(Larus marinus)*
  herring *(Larus argentatus)*
  laughing *(Larus atricilla)*
  lesser black-backed *(Larus fuscus)*
  little *(Larus minutus)*
  ring-billed *(Larus delawarensis)*
  Sabine's *(Xema sabini)*

hawk, marsh *(Circus cyaneus)*
heron, black-crowned night *(Nycticorax nycticorax)*
  yellow-crowned night *(Nyctanassa violacea)*
  great blue *(Ardea herodias)*
  green *(Butorides virescens)*
  little blue *(Florida caerulea)*
  Louisiana *(Hydranassa tricolor)*

ibis, glossy *(Plegadis falcinellus)*

jay, blue *(Cyanocitta cristata)*

killdeer *(Charadrius vociferus)*
kingfisher, belted *(Megaceryle alcyon)*
kinglet, golden-crowned *(Regulus satrapa)*
  ruby-crowned *(Regulus calendula)*
kittiwake, black-legged *(Rissa tridactyla)*
knot *(Calidris canutus)*

mallard *(Anas platyrhynchos)*
merganser, hooded *(Lophodytes cucullatus)*
  red-breasted *(Mergus serrator)*
mockingbird *(Mimus polyglottos)*

nuthatch, brown-headed *(Sitta pusilla)*
  red-breasted *(Sitta canadensis)*
  white-breasted *(Sitta carolinensis)*

old-squaw *(Clangula hyemalis)*
oriole, Baltimore *(Icterus galbula)*
osprey *(Pandion haliaetus)*
owl, saw-whet *(Aegolius acadicus)*
    snowy *(Nyctea scandiaca)*

parakeet, Carolina *(Conuropsis carolinensis)*
pheasant, ring-necked *(Phasianus colchicus)*
pigeon, passenger *(Ectopistes migratorius)*
pintail *(Anas acuta)*
plover, black-bellied *(Squatarola squatarola)*

reedbird *(Dolichonyx oryzivorus)*
rail, black *(Laterallus jamaicensis)*
    clapper *(Rallus longirostris)*
    king *(Rallus elegans)*
    sora *(Porzana carolina)*
    Virginia *(Rallus limicola)*
    yellow *(Coturnicops noveboracensis)*
redhead *(Aythya americana)*
redstart *(Setophaga ruticilla)*

scaup *(Aythya marila* and *Aythya affinis)*
scoter, common *(Oidemia nigra)*
    surf *(Melanitta perspicillata)*
    white-winged *(Melanitta deglandi)*
shoveler *(Spatula clypeata)*
skimmer, black *(Rynchops nigra)*
snipe, common *(Capella gallinago)*
sora *(Porzana carolina)*
sparrow, house *(Passer domesticus)*
    seaside *(Ammospiza maritima)*
    sharp-tailed *(Ammospiza caudacuta)*
    song *(Melospiza melodia)*
    swamp *(Melospiza georgiana)*

swan, whistling *(Olor columbianus)*
swallow, bank *(Riparia riparia)*
teal, blue-winged *(Anas discors)*
    green-winged *(Anas carolinensis)*
tern, least *(Sterna albifrons)*
    sooty *(Sterna fuscata)*
titmouse, tufted *(Parus bicolor)*
tropic bird, white-tailed *(Phaethon lepturus)*
vulture, turkey *(Cathartes aura)*

warbler, hooded *(Wilsonia pusilla)*
    myrtle *(Dendroica coronata)*
    parula *(Parula americana)*
    pine *(Dendroica pinus)*
    prothonotary *(Protonotaria citrea)*
    Swainson's *(Limnothlypis swainsonii)*
    worm-eating *(Helmitheros vermivorus)*
    yellow *(Dendroica petchia)*
    yellow-throated *(Dendroica dominica)*
water thrush, Louisiana *(Seiurus motacilla)*
whimbrel *(Numenius phaeopus)*
whippoorwill *(Caprimulgus vociferus)*
widgeon, American *(Mareca americana)*
willet *(Catoptrophorus semipalmatus)*
woodcock *(Philohela minor)*
woodpecker, downy *(Dendrocopos
    pubescens)*
    red-cockaded *(Dendrocopos borealis)*
wren, long-billed marsh *(Telmatodytes
    palustris)*
    short-billed marsh *(Cistothorus platensis)*

yellowlegs, greater *(Totanus melanoleucus)*
    lesser *(Totanus flavipes)*

Common and Scientific Names of Plants

alder, common *(Alnus serrulata)*
    seaside *(Alnus maritima)*
arrow-arum *(Peltandra virginica)*
arrowhead *(Sagittaria* sp.)

black grass *(Juncus gerardi)*
black rush *(Juncus roemerianus)*
bulrush, river *(Scirpus fluviatilis)*
    salt-marsh *(Scirpus robustus)*
    soft-stem *(Scirpus validus)*
bur reed *(Sparganium* sp.)
butterweed *(Bidens* sp.)

cattail, broadleaf *(Typha latifolia)*
    narrowleaf *(Typha angustifolia)*
cherry, wild *(Prunus* sp.)
climbing hempweed *(Mikania scandens)*
cordgrass, big *(Spartina cynosuroides)*
    salt-marsh *(Spartina alterniflora)*
    salt-meadow *(Spartina patens)*
corn *(Zea mays)*
cross vine *(Bignonia capreolata)*
cut-grass, giant *(Zizaniopsis mileacea)*
    rice *(Leersia oryzoides)*

cypress, bald *(Taxodium distichum)*

dayflower, Asiatic *(Aneilema keisak)*
dogwood *(Cornus florida)*
   silky *(Cornus amomum)*

eelgrass *(Zostera marina)*

grape *(Vitis* sp.*)*
grass, foxtail *(Setaria* sp.*)*
greenbrier *(Smilax)*
groundsel bush *(Baccharis halimifolia)*
gum, black *(Nyssa sylvatica)*
   sweet *(Liquidambar styraciflua)*

hackberry *(Celtis occidentalis)*
hibiscus, marsh *(Hibiscus moscheutos)*
horse sugar *(Symplocus tinctoria)*
high-tide bush *(Iva frutescens)*

jewelweed *(Impatiens* sp.*)*

lobelia *(Lobelia* sp.*)*

magnolia, swamp *(Magnolia virginiana)*
mallow, rose *(Hibiscus moscheutos)*
   salt-marsh *(Kosteletzkya virginica)*
maple, red *(Acer rubrum)*
millet, Walter *(Echinochloa walteri)*
myrtle, wax *(Myrica cerifera)*

needlerush *(Juncus roemerianus)*

oak, water *(Quercus nigra)*
   white *(Quercus alba)*

peanut *(Arachis hypogaea)*

pepper bush, sweet *(Clethra alnifolia)*
phragmites *(Phragmites communis)*
pickerelweed *(Pontederia cordata)*
pine, loblolly *(Pinus taeda)*
pondweeds *(Potamogeton* spp.*)*

ragweed *(Ambrosia* sp.*)*
rice, domestic *(Oryza sativa)*
rose, swamp *(Rosa palustris)*

salt grass *(Distichilis spicata)*
sea lettuce *(Ulva lactuca)*
sedges *(Cyperus* spp.*)*
smartweed, dotted *(Polygonum punctatum)*
soft rush *(Juncus effusus)*
sorghum *(Sorghum vulgare)*
spike rush, dwarf *(Eleocharis parvula)*
sweet flag *(Acorus calamus)*
switch grass *(Panicum virgatum)*
sycamore *(Platanus occidentalis)*

tearthumb, arrowleaf *(Polygonum sagittatum)*
   halberdleaf *(Polygonum arifolium)*
three-square, common *(Scirpus americanus)*
   Olney *(Scirpus olneyi)*

water hemp, tidemarsh *(Acnida cannabina)*
water parsnip *(Sium suave)*
wheat *(Triticum aestivum)*
widgeon grass *(Ruppia maritima)*
wild celery *(Vallisneria americana)*
wild rice *(Zizania aquatica)*
wool grass *(Scirpus cyperinus)*

Common and Scientific Names of Mammals

cottontail, eastern *(Silvilagus floridanus)*
fox, red *(Vulpes fulva)*

mouse *(Peromyscus* sp.*)*
muskrat *(Ondatra zibethica)*

raccoon *(Procyon lotor)*

rat, cotton *(Sigmodon hispidus)*
   rice *(Oryzomys palustris)*

shrew *(Sorex* sp.*)*
skunk *(Mephitis mephitis)*
squirrel, Delmarva fox *(Sciurus niger bryanti)*

vole, meadow *(Microtus pennsylvanicus)*

Common and Scientific Names of Other Animals

armyworm, fall *(Laphygma frugiperda)*

clam, long ("soft-shelled") *(Mya arenaria)*
   macoma *(Macoma balthica)*
   rangia *(Rangia cuneata)*

crab, common fiddler *(Uca* sp.)
   red-jointed fiddler *(Uca minax)*
   square-backed fiddler *(Sesarma
     reticulatum)*

crayfish *(Cambarus* sp.)

cricket *(Gryllidae)*

dragonfly nymphs *(Anisoptera)*

frog *(Rana* sp.)

grasshopper *(Orthoptera)*

killifish *(Fundulus heteroclitus)*

shrimp *(Peneus setiferus?)*

snail *(Amnicola* sp.)
   periwinkle *(Littorina* sp.)
   salt-marsh *(Melampus bidentatus)*

snake, red-bellied water *(Natrix
    erythrogaster erythrogaster)*
   water *(Natrix* sp.)

terrapin, diamond-backed *(Malaclemys
    terrapin terrapin)*

worm, marine *(Nereis* sp.)

BIBLIOGRAPHY

(1) Meanley, B., 1965. Early-fall food and habitat of the sora in the Patuxent River marsh, Maryland. *Chesapeake Science*, 6:235-237.

(2) Blogg, P.T., 1944. *There are no dull dark days.* H.G. Roebuck and Son. Baltimore, Maryland. 92 p.

(3) Swales, B.W., 1896. A "Full Set of Rails." *Nidiologist,* 3:142.

(4) Abbott, J.M., 1973. Bald eagle nest survey, 1973. *Atlantic Naturalist,* 28:158-159.

(5) Bent, A.C., 1937. *Life histories of North American birds of prey.* Part 1. U.S. National Museum Bulletin 167. Smithsonian Institution, Washington, D.C., 409 p.

(6) Smith, F., 1938. *Muskrat investigations in Dorchester County, Maryland, 1930-34.* U.S.D.A. Circular No. 474, Washington, D.C., 24 p.

(7) Abbott, J.M., 1971. Bald eagle nest survey, 1971. *Atlantic Naturalist,* 26:165-166.

(8) Bureau of Sport Fisheries and Wildlife, 1968. *Wildlife research—problems, programs, progress.* U.S. Department of the Interior, Washington, D.C. 51-52.

(9) Stewart, R.E., and C.S. Robbins, 1958. *Birds of Maryland and the District of Columbia.* North American Fauna 62. U.S. Department of the Interior. 401 p.

(10) Bent, A.C., 1948. *Life histories of North American nuthatches, wrens, thrashers and their allies.* U.S. National Museum Bulletin 195. Smithsonian Institution, Washington, D.C., 475 p.

(11) Blogg, P.T., 1946. Bobolink (Reedbird). *Rally Sheet.* League of Maryland Sportsmen, Baltimore. 3:7.

(12) Audubon, J.J., 1835. *Ornithological biography,* volume 3. Adam and Charles Black, Edinburg, Scotland. 631 p.

(13) Meanley, B., and R.E. Stewart, 1960. Color of the tarsi and toes of the black rail. *Auk,* 77:83-84.

(14) Wright, P.L., and M.H. Wright, 1944. The reproductive cycle of the male red-winged blackbird. *Condor,* 46:46-59.

(15) Henny, C.J., M.M. Smith and V.D. Stotts, 1974. The 1973 distribution and abundance of breeding ospreys in the Chesapeake Bay. *Chesapeake Science,* 15:125-133.

(16) Wiley, J.W., and F.E. Lohrer, 1973. Additional records of non-fish prey taken by ospreys. *Wilson Bulletin,* 85:468-470.

(17) Reese, J., 1970. Reproduction in a Chesapeake Bay osprey population. *Auk,* 87:747-759.

(18) Reese, J., 1973. Nesting success of Chesapeake Bay ospreys in 1973. *Maryland Birdlife,* 29:105-106.

(19) Henny, C.J., and H.M. Wight, 1969. An endangered osprey population: estimates of mortality and production. *Auk,* 82:188-198.

(20) Reese, J., 1969. A Maryland osprey population 75 years ago and today. *Maryland Birdlife*, 25:116-119.

(21) Harris, V.T., 1953. Ecological relationships of meadow voles and rice rats in tidal marshes. *Journal of Mammalogy*, 34:479-487.

(22) Stotts, V.D., and D.E. Davis, 1960. The black duck in the Chesapeake Bay of Maryland: breeding behavior and biology. *Chesapeake Science*, 1:127-154.

(23) Tomkins, I.R., 1958. *The birdlife of the Savannah River delta*. Occasional Paper No. 4, Georgia Ornithological Society. 68 p.

(24) Stewart, R.E., 1945. Migratory movements of the northern clapper rail. *Bird-Banding*, 25:1-5.

(25) Bond, G., and R.E. Stewart, 1951. A new swamp sparrow from the Maryland coastal plain. *Wilson Bulletin*, 63:38-40.

(26) Steirly, C.C., 1957. Nesting ecology of the red-cockaded woodpecker in Virginia. *Atlantic Naturalist*, 12:280-292.

(27) Scott, F.R., 1969. Bird observations from the Northern Neck. *Raven*, 40:67-80.

(28) Norris, R.A., 1958. *Comparative biosystematics and life history of nuthatches Sitta pygmaea and Sitta pusilla*. University of California Publication in Zoology, 56:119-300. University of California Press, Berkley and Los Angeles.

(29) Hickey, M.B., 1954. 54th Christmas bird count (southern Dorchester County, Maryland). *Audubon Field Notes*, 8:103.

(30) Meanley, B., 1971. *Natural history of the Swainson's warbler*. North American Fauna 69. U.S. Department of the Interior. 90 p.

(31) Stewart, R.E., A.D. Geis and C.D. Evans, 1958. Distribution of populations and hunting kill of the canvasback. *Journal of Wildlife Management*, 22:333-370.

(32) Bystrak, P.G., 1974. The Maryland Christmas counts of 1973. *Maryland Birdlife*, 30:3-7.

(33) Springer, P. and R.E. Stewart, 1950. Gadwall nesting in Maryland. *Auk*, 67:234-235.

(34) Armistead, H.T., 1970. First Maryland breeding of coot at Deal Island. *Maryland Birdlife*, 26:79-81.

(35) Armistead, H.T., 1971. First Maryland breeding of the green-winged teal. *Maryland Birdlife*, 27:111-114.

(36) Armistead, H.T., 1974. Lower Chesapeake heronries of Maryland Smith Island to Barren Island. *Maryland Birdlife*, 30:9-27.

(37) Stewart, R.E., 1962. *Waterfowl populations in the upper Chesapeake Region*. U.S. Department of the Interior—Fish and Wildlife Service, Special Scientific Report—Wildlife no. 65. Washington, D.C. 208 p.

(38) Martin, A.C. and F.M. Uhler, 1951. *Food of game ducks in the United States and Canada*. Research Report 30. Fish and Wildlife Service, U.S. Department of the Interior. Washington, D.C. 308 p.

(39) Catesby, M., 1731-43. *The natural history of Carolina, Florida and the Bahama Islands*. 2 volumes. London.

(40) Murray, J.J., 1952. *A check-list of the birds of Virginia.* The Virginia Society of Ornithology. 113 p.

(41) Bent, A.C., 1940. *Life histories of North American cuckoos, goatsuckers, hummingbirds and their allies.* U.S. National Museum Bulletin 176. Smithsonian Institution, Washington, D.C. 506 p.

(42) Stone, W., 1929. Mark Catesby and the nomenclature of North American birds. *Auk*, 46:447-454.

(43) Buckley, P.A. and F.G. Buckley, 1967. The current status of certain birds in the Virginia Capes area. I. Fall and Winter 1966-1967. *Raven*, 38:39-45.

(44) Buckley, P.A., and F.G. Buckley, 1968. Current status of certain birds in the Virginia Capes area. II. April 1967-July 1968 observations. *Raven*, 39:27-40.

(45) Reese, J., 1966. An unprecedented concentration of saw-whet owls. *Maryland Birdlife*, 22:31.

(46) Gross, A.O., 1927. The snowy owl migrations of 1926-27. *Auk*, 44:479-493.

(47) Kenny, F.L., 1969. Time for another snowy owl invasion? *Insight.* U.S. Bureau of Sport Fisheries and Wildlife. p. 2.

INDEX

Hudson Bay, 64
Hurricane Agnes, 118
Incubation period, 30
  king rail, 20
Indians, Chippewa, 2

Jamaica, 40
James Bay, 62
James River, 120, 125, 130, 131
  Country, 124, 132, 134
Jamestown, 124, 125, 126, 127, 128,
  129, 130, 133
Jay, blue, 48
Jones, Bob, 133
Julian, Bill, 67

Kenny, Frank L., 141
Kent County, 56
Kent Island, Maryland, 46, 121, 136
Kent Point, 135
Kentuck Swamp, 57
Key West, 68
Killifish, 9
King George County, Va., 100, 103, 118
Kinglets, golden-crowned, 94
King rail
  (*See* Rail, king)
Kiptopeake, Va., 98
Kirkwood, Frank, 56
Kleen, Vernon, 97
Klimkiewicz, Kathy, 141

Lake Okeechobee, 40
Lark, horned, 46
Life Histories of North American Birds,
  26
Lohrer, F.E., 53
Lord Baltimore, 1
Louisiana, 33, 59
Lyon's Creek, 1, 9

Maine, 68
Manokin River, 104, 120
Marshes
  brackish, 41, 122
  Brackish Estuarine Bay type, 58
  cattail, 20, 32, 65, 67
  fresh tidal, 1, 9
  Nanticoke, 82
  needlerush, 67, 104, 106, 107
  Olney three-square, 14, 15, 42, 59, 65,
    67, 82, 122
  rice, 36, 38, 39, 125, 138
  rush, 19
  salt-marsh meadow, 59, 67
  (*See also* Plants, aquatic; Rice, wild-)

Marsh hen (*See* Rail, king; Rail, clapper)
Marshyhope Creek, 83
Martin, A.C., 122
Marumsco Creek, 104, 108
Maryland Birdlife, 56, 110, 136
Mattaponi River, 122
McLauchlin, Dave, 63
Meanley, B., 142
Middle Atlantic States, 23, 39, 93
Middle River, 30
Migration, 10, 11, 12
  blackbird, 38, 46
  marsh wren, 35
  rail, 23, 41
  reedbird, 36, 37-38
  routes, 115
  teal, blue-winged, 61
  warbler, 98
  woodcock, 67
Mississippi Valley, 40, 77
Mitchell, Robert, 139
Mobjack Bay, 120
Molluscs, 69
Molting season, 11
  rail, 22
  reedbird, 36
Moneystump, 57
Morgantown, Maryland, 27, 28
"Mudding," 75
Muskrat, 4, 12, 14, 16, 28, 42, 58, 82
  "eatout," 43, 61
  food, 59
  trails, 15
  trappers, 60

Nansemond River, 127, 128, 130, 131
Nanticoke River, 15, 39, 41, 79, 80, 81,
  82, 83, 85, 86, 122
National Audubon Society, 65
Nest
  bittern, 31
  canvasback, 102
  chuck-will's-widow, 90
  climber's equipment, 26
  construction, 25
  eagle, 24, 25, 26, 28, 29
  nuthatch, 91, 94
  rail, 19, 20, 21, 74
  reedbird, 36
  warbler, 97
  willet, 73
Nesting season, 18, 30, 42, 46
  blackbird, 49-51
  eagle, 46